EVALUATING A COURSE

The Complete Guide to Teaching a Course
Ian Forsyth, Alan Jolliffe and David Stevens

Planning a Course
Preparing a Course
Delivering a Course
Evaluating a Course

EVALUATING A COURSE

Practical Strategies for Teachers, Lecturers and Trainers

Ian Forsyth, Alan Jolliffe and David Stevens

First published in 1995

Kogan Page Limited
120 Pentonville Road
London N1 9JN

British Library Cataloguing in Publication Data
A CIP record for this book is available from the British Library.

ISBN 0 7494 1530 4

Typeset by BookEns Ltd, Royston, Herts.
Printed and bound in Great Britain by Biddles Ltd, Guildford and King's Lynn

Contents

Introduction

WHAT IS THIS BOOK ALL ABOUT?

This book is about the evaluation of courses, course support materials and their presentation to learners. It also considers the outcomes to the learner and the community of the learner. It is the fourth in the series on planning, preparing, delivering and evaluating new courses and course materials.

In *Planning a Course* the systematic collection of information about the course, the clients, and the learners is considered. In other words, what is the course going to do, with who, for what outcomes and with what resources.

In *Preparing a Course* the issues involved in the preparation to deliver instructional materials were addressed. It would be difficult to address all of these but there are 'generic' issues such as the mode of delivery of a course, selecting pre-produced materials and dealing with the production of new course support materials.

The third book, *Delivering a Course,* looked at various issues in the delivery of course materials, and extended to asking you to consider the various audiences that could see themselves as part of the educational and training community.

The focus in this book is on evaluation. As far as possible the term 'evaluation' is allied to learning materials. The terms 'test' and 'assessment' are allied to the tasks and outcomes for the learners.

WHAT DOES EACH CHAPTER COVER?

Chapter 1 reviews how evaluation data can be used to ensure course materials and delivery methodologies are doing the job they were designed to do. It also presents an overview of each of the four levels of assessment and how each can be used to the benefit of the teacher and the learner.

Learning takes place in an 'environment'. Chapter 2 outlines some of the environmental factors you may need to consider.

Chapter 3 asks: What is wrong with qualitative assessment? Many people seem to think that you have to have statistics. What is wrong with recording the smiles on the faces?

As Chapter 4 points out, we talk about knowledge, skills and attitudes or the taxonomy of the cognitive, affective and the psychomotor domains. But for most learners the question is: Did we pass and what was the mark? Other stakeholders may want to know: Does this person know their work?; while teachers may want to question what are some of the possibilities of evaluation of students' work.

The subject of Chapter 5 is the iterative evaluation process. Each time you offer a course it is the first time for the students. Yet each offering of a course may see teachers wanting to alter the course or materials in the light of experience. These alterations need to be systematic and documented.

Chapter 6 looks at the outcome for the learner. How do you determine the effect of the course, your presentation, or whether other influences had effect? So students seem to have learned, but what was it in the materials that facilitated this process, and what hindered learning? Will these factors be the same the next time around?

Chapter 7 discusses what the results of the course might mean to you. What do you do with the results, and what follow up might take place? Chapter 8 then reinforces aspects of evaluating course and materials, helping you to continuously improve the product you have developed.

We hope you find the materials in this book interesting and useful. Happy reading and evaluating.

Ian R Forsyth
Alan K Jolliffe
David I Stevens
Singapore 1995

Chapter 1
Course And Materials Evaluation

▶ **SUMMARY** 

The evaluation of a learning event, learning materials or an educational innovation can be used to assist you to better understand the learning environment in which you are working. This environment includes the institution, the classroom, the learning materials, the use of media, delivery methodologies and administration. It also includes the learner's belief as to the overall effectiveness of the institution, the learning event or the learning materials being used. This chapter is an overview of each of the four 'levels' of evaluation: reaction, learning, behaviour change and results to the organization, and of their strengths, limitations and use in a learning setting.

INTRODUCTION

To evaluate is to appraise, assess, estimate or ascertain the amount of something. Evaluation is the act of doing these things with respect to making a judgement regarding the worth or value of that something.

A review of evaluation suggests that the process is divided into two parts. The first is a formative procedure directed toward those decisions you have to make regarding the various processes related to learning event management, and the second is a summative procedure directed toward those decisions you have to make about the learning event as a whole. You can consider the outcome of the first procedure as learning event modification. The outcome of the second procedure may also be learning event modification; however its primary function is to help you address issues of learning event continuance.

Evaluation should never be an afterthought. Make it part of your planning at the outset.

At least five broad areas of concern can be identified for evaluation purposes. These are: statistical measurement; learner congruence between their performance and the objectives set out for each portion of the learning materials; professional judgement; description and judgement; and information for decision making.

This chapter reviews the development and administration of evaluation with respect to the four levels of evaluation as defined by Kirkpatrick (1977).

EVALUATION MODEL

There are many evaluation models that can be used in various learning environments. The Kirkpatrick model, developed in the early 1970s, has stood the test of time and stands out in terms of overall simplicity and ease of administration. Furthermore, Kirkpatrick's model addresses both summative

Table 1.1 *Model overview*

Level	Evaluation context	Data collection
Level 1 REACTION	This evaluation is a measurement of the learner's feelings and opinions about the course just completed.	The type of information collected here relates to methods of instruction, course content and institution, learning materials and facilities.
Level 2 LEARNING	This evaluation is a measurement of what has been learned as a result of the learning event. It examines the facts, skills and attitudes the learner has gained from the event.	The type of information collected here relates to the learner's achievement of the learning event objectives.
Level 3 BEHAVIOURAL CHANGES	This evaluation is a measurement of the behavioural changes occurring as a result of the learning event just completed.	The type of information collected here examines individual learner behaviour/ performance after the learning event. It looks at the changes that can occur and the impact of those changes in a new situation.
Level 4 RESULTS TO THE ORGANIZATION	This evaluation is a measurement of the overall impact of an innovation on the institutional environment.	The type of information collected here relates to costs, improvement of employee morale, turnover rates and productivity on a total institutional basis.

and formative evaluation - with which you, as part of the education and training community, should concern yourself.

The Kirkpatrick model outlines four levels of evaluation and suggests that a number of different evaluative tasks have to take place at each level. This indicates that as the impact of the evaluation on learning events, the learners, the administration and the facility becomes apparent, so the tasks have to change to ensure the validity of the evaluative procedure.

THE EVALUATION CONTEXT

That you should evaluate your various learning events or learning materials needs no discussion. The decision that you will need to make is which level of evaluation you should use to ensure that the learning event or materials in question retain their high standards. Most institutions have a serious commitment to Level 2 or learning evaluation; however, it is difficult to determine what, if any, evaluation is carried out at other levels. A strong argument could be made for the use of a Level 3 evaluation to determine the extent of the behavioural change with learners involved in a co-operative education programme, for example, or with teaching staff after they have completed teacher training. A case could also be made for conducting a Level 4 evaluation across all institutional departments to review the viability of an innovation. However, research indicates that the inherent difficulties of such an undertaking may result in less than positive results.

LEVEL 1

Reaction to the learning event or the learning materials

Level 1 is the simplest form of evaluation. It should be considered during the planning process.

Measuring the reaction to your learning event or learning materials at Level 1 involves an evaluation of the learner's feelings and opinions about the materials to which they have just been exposed. It is important to emphasize that this reaction is *not* a measurement of the learning that may or may not have taken place. However, learning theories strongly suggest that if learners are interested and enthusiastic about the subject they are more likely to internalize the material presented during the learning event.

Evaluation characteristics

Generally a Level 1 evaluation is carried out by you or an independent evaluator either during a learning event or just after its completion. Level 1 evaluations accomplish two things: first they provide feedback on issues affecting learning events and/or the effectiveness of learning materials' effectiveness and second, they encourage learners to share responsibility for their own learning. Evaluation at Level 1 should be as non-threatening and as efficient as possible. If too high an emphasis is placed on the evaluation it can have an impact on how the learning event itself is perceived by the learners.

Level 1 evaluation can be used to assist in appraising yourself as a teacher, or other teachers, the facility, the learner's belief as to the effectiveness of the learning event, the use of media, the pace at which the materials were delivered, the delivery methodologies and administration.

It is important that you understand that the results of a Level 1 evaluation can be subject to a number of variables such as the duration and learning event content. The most important variable however is the personality and personal dynamics of the teacher. A very dynamic teacher may actually be less effective than someone less intense. A viable Level 1 evaluation instrument should therefore focus on the content of the learning event rather than the personality of the teacher.

Two general approaches can be used to gather the necessary data; one oral, the other written. Whichever method you use, the compilation of results is simplified when you use some form of scale. A purely subjective instrument will make it difficult for you to average results and summarize comments. But if you develop an instrument or methodology that focuses only on answers to direct questions, you may be deprived of possible solutions that could be provided by learners who perceive a deficiency in the learning event.

Conditions necessary for successful evaluation

Since learners are supplying information regarding their personal reactions to a learning event, it is important that they feel protected. If a written evaluation method is used, individuals should be able to remain anonymous if they so choose. If an oral method is used, you should adhere to the general rules for accepting feedback: listen, thank the learner, and avoid defensive behaviour.

A learner's smile of achievement is evidence that things are going well.

It is also important that your data collection instrument focuses on those educational activities that support your learning event and the physical aspects of the facility as perceived by the learners. Failure to do so can result in your evaluation being reduced to a 'happiness index', which simply asks learners how they liked the learning event. One result of a 'happiness' form of evaluation is that it is sometimes difficult to generalize to the population, because the suggestions are often self-cancelling.

It is important therefore that you design something that is more than a happiness index. You must decide what you wish to evaluate and then design the questions that will assist the learner in supplying you with this information. Keep in mind that compiling large amounts of written responses to short-answer questions is a time-consuming process and you really should consider using some form of scale or rating system to quantify reaction.

Since the data are self-reported, you will need to provide a structure to assist the learners to focus their comments. Your questions should be clear and able to be answered either briefly, or marked on some form of scale such as the Likert scale or answered using a simple 'yes' or 'no'.

Likert scales are a popular method of choice and usually employ five choices expressing different degrees of agreement or disagreement that yield ordinal measurements (SA = strongly agree, A = agree, N = not sure, D = disagree, and SD = strongly disagree). Using this method your statements are never neutral but favourable or unfavourable to a certain degree. The scores are computed by weighting the responses from five to one for a favourable statement beginning with strong agreement. This is reversed for unfavourable statements. For example, consider the following two questions taken from a questionnaire designed to measure the learner's response to a learning event.

The objectives of the learning event were clearly explained by the teacher:	SA A N D SD
My participation in the role plays was not a valuable experience for me:	SA A N D SD

If the respondent agrees with the first statement and circles the A, a statement becomes one that is favourable to the learning event so it is assigned a value of four. However, if the respondent circles the A in the second statement, it becomes a negative response to the learning event so it is given a reverse score of two.

Keep your reaction questionnaire to one or at most two pages and leave space for the respondent to comment.

When you are designing your questionnaire remember that learning theory suggests that people have difficulty making decisions and judgements based on scales of more than five choices.

Strengths

A Level 1 evaluation that uses a large sample from the population avoids the possibility that changes will be made to learning events based on the comments and impact of a few vocal individuals who are either extremely satisfied or unsatisfied with the learning event. A Level 1 evaluation can assist you in examining the effect of existing organization and administration on the learner and help you to uncover the reasons behind certain kinds of behaviours. Failure to deal with learner concerns can be extremely costly in terms of dissatisfaction towards other learning events, facilities and other people. If you administer a Level 1 questionnaire midway through a learning event it could help you to make the next part of the event or subsequent events more effective. As noted previously, if learners generally like a learning event, they are more likely to obtain maximum benefit from it. A Level 1 evaluation will also provide you with the opportunity to examine the impact that your colleagues have on the same or similar groups.

Finally, a Level 1 evaluation provides learners with an immediate opportunity to become involved in providing input to decisions made during their learning process. This may result in a feeling of increased involvement and has the potential to increase support for your learning event.

Limitations

The first limitation of a Level I evaluation is that it does *not* measure any changes in what has been learned. Second, the impact of the individual teacher can taint the instrument. The same caution also applies to all other components being evaluated. For example, if the classroom is deemed unsatisfactory this may result in learners downgrading the scores they give other things. If oral evaluation methods are used, it is possible for very vocal learners to dominate the group during debriefing sessions. In some cases, because they are easier to identify and associate, the negative aspects of a learning event are described - often to the detriment of observing the positive points.

Methods of administration

Three methodologies can be used to administer a Level 1 evaluation in an educational setting. These are:

1. An oral evaluation administered in a classroom setting.
2. A written evaluation also administered in the classroom.
3. Individual interviews with learners conducted outside of the classroom.

You can carry out an oral evaluation either during or at the conclusion of the learning event, and the questionnaires and interviews can be completed during, at the conclusion of, or following the learning event. Because of the time-consuming nature of post-learning event interviews and the number of people you will have to get to help you conduct the interview, this methodology is not considered appropriate for use in many institutional settings.

LEVEL 2

Level 2 evaluation is the determination of what has been learned as a result of a learning event. This may include the learner's attainment of the learning objectives and assessment of changes in knowledge, skills, and attitudes. While Level 1 examined how the learning was received by the learner, Level 2 evaluation focuses on what has been learned. However it is important to understand that there is a difference between the skills learned and skills that can be demonstrated in another setting. Level 2 evaluation can only examine the skills that the learner is able to demonstrate in the learning setting and this is *not* a guarantee that it is transferable to other settings. (The technique for developing and administering a Level 1 evaluation is covered in detail in Chapter 2.)

Characteristics

There are a number of reasons for evaluating at Level 2. These include the need for quantifiable data about a learning event or learning materials, or to determine if the learning objectives were achieved. Also, a Level 2 evaluation can provide information to the learners about their progress and provide information about a learner's progress to the institution. Finally, a Level 2 evaluation can give information which will allow you to improve the learning event or learning materials and assess whether or not specific parts of your materials have structural defects that need to be corrected. You must also consider planning for a Level 2 evaluation if there is a need to certify learners upon completion of the learning event.

A Level 2 evaluation is a test or examination.

For each of the three areas assessed by Level 2 - changes in knowledge, attitudes, and skills - a pre-test/post-test and control group design can be used, so that any changes in learning can be attributed to the learning event. This design should include using the same measurement before and after the event, measuring those who have taken advantage of the learning event against those who have not, and randomly assigning individuals to learning events and control groups.

Strengths

The major strength of a Level 2 evaluation is that it is easier to measure the learning that has taken place than to measure learner performance in a setting different to that in which the learning happened. Quantifiable data can be easily obtained, and depending on your needs, rigorous adherence to scientific method can provide the institution with data that are statistically defensible. Knowledge gain measurements have more rigour than other instruments because they are not easy to falsify. You also have a high degree of control of the evaluation at Level 2, since it often takes place during the learning event.

Limitations

Although you can infer transfer of learning to another setting, an increase in knowledge or change in attitude does not necessarily ensure an increase in performance on the part of the learner. A second limitation is that learners can have a negative response to some of the evaluation methods because they have an aversion to being tested.

Methods of administration

Pencil and paper tests such as multiple choice questions, short-answer tests, true and false tests, or matching items, are useful methods for assessing knowledge. Multiple choice testing is probably one of the better methods to use for assessing principles and facts. It is among the most objective forms of testing and can measure higher orders of learning, such as understanding, judgement, and application of knowledge. The method is often superior to other objective test methods since these other methods can encourage guessing, often provide clues, and for the most part test lower learning levels such as memorization. Short-answer and essay questions are also less effective because of their subjective nature, the time needed to complete and mark them and because they often test unrelated skills such as spelling that can penalize learners who cannot express themselves clearly in writing. Measuring skills can be carried out using behaviour checklists, role plays, or actual performance in the learning setting. Attitude change can be measured using questionnaires, attitude surveys, interviews, informal observation, and self-rating scales.

The construction of test items is a difficult and critical task and a great deal of experience on the part of the teacher is needed to develop questions that measure at the higher levels of the cognitive domain and to ensure that incorrect responses are not obvious. Testing should, of course, follow as soon as possible after the learning event as any delay could result in outside influences affecting the scores.

LEVEL 3

Evaluation Levels 1 and 2 look at the learner's reaction to the learning event or learning materials and whether they gained any new knowledge, skills, or attitudes. Level 3 evaluation measures the extent to which the learners are now able to apply what they have learned in a different setting. Here you are seeking to measure changes in behaviour or increases in level of performance. Level 3 evaluation is especially important in training and is concerned with the impact of the training on real-life situations. The issue here is that understanding the concept or applying a skill in a learning setting does not automatically guarantee that the learner has the ability to transfer it to a new situation.

Characteristics

Level 3 evaluation is characterized by measures that take place outside the setting of the learning event. Since the intent is to measure the impact of new behaviour in a different setting the evaluation must take place in the learner's place of work. Because of this, the evaluation also involves a wider variety of people than do Levels 1 and 2, which typically involve only learners and possibly just yourself. Designing a Level 3 evaluation can be time-consuming and implementation may be complex.

Conditions necessary for successful evaluation

It has been noted by many writers that measuring changes in a person's behaviour can be a difficult and frustrating process since a number of significant requirements are needed in order for change to take place. It is extremely important that you consider each of the following conditions prior to designing your Level 3 evaluation scheme.

1. The learners must want to improve themselves.
2. The learners must recognize their own learning deficiencies.
3. The learners must work in a receptive organizational climate.
4. The learners will need help from someone else who is interested and skilled in that area of learning.
5. The learners must have the opportunity to try out the new ideas.

You should consider using a Level 3 evaluation when your major concern is to provide evidence or proof regarding the effectiveness of the learning event. It is possible to evaluate at Level 3 without evaluating at Level 2. However, it may be useful to evaluate at both Levels 2 and 3 as you may discover that while knowledge is being gained by learners during the learning events, the environment in another setting is not conducive to the changed behaviour. This becomes especially important if the rationale for the learning event is being questioned because of some perceived failure, when the real reason is an environment that does not support the learner but discourages or extinguishes new behaviour.

Strengths

Level 3 evaluation will provide more meaningful information about the work place than a Level 2 evaluation and may bring about an increased commitment to innovation. One of the consequences of a Level 3 evaluation can be the change in the focus of a learning event from teacher-centred to that of learner-centred.

Limitations

By measuring individual behaviour you may be measuring how the five conditions - statistical measurement; learner congruence between their performance and the objectives set out for each portion of the learning materials; professional judgement; description and judgement; and information for decision making - are met, rather than measuring the quality of the learning event.

When planning an evaluation, remember that it may take the learner many weeks to put learning into practice.

Level 3 evaluation is more time-consuming than a Level 1 evaluation and more difficult to implement than a Level 2 evaluation. Learners may not react as positively to involvement in a Level 3 evaluation due to the more observational nature of the evaluation. However, because more people are involved in the evaluation it is important that the organization be carefully prepared for the event. Because evaluation must be done after individuals have had a chance to demonstrate behaviour, longer time lines are an inevitable result. In addition, if the learning event is attempting to teach a skill that is used infrequently there may be a significant time-lag before you are able to measure the effectiveness of the learning event on the behaviour.

LEVEL 4

In order to determine if an innovation has been successful, it is necessary to conduct an evaluation at Level 4. Level 4 evaluation is concerned with linking any changes in the organization to a recent innovation. Although Level 4 is a desirable level of evaluation because it represents a truly indicative measure of the outcome of an innovation to the organization, it is the most difficult and time-consuming to conduct. Change in an organization can be the result of a number of factors, and it is the role of the evaluator to link the change to the innovation but at the same time try to eliminate all other variables as factors in that change. The task requires the total support and commitment of everyone involved. There is no set formula or process that applies to Level 4. To determine if the innovation did result in the perceived change, it may be necessary to use control groups. The use of control groups in large organizations, however, is not always practical and you may have to use other methods to gather the evidence you need.

Characteristics

A Level 4 evaluation can provide the data you need to make an informed judgement about an innovation.

Level 4 evaluation concerns the net effect of an innovation on an organization. It helps measure the overall costs of an innovation and improvement in people. In a training setting it can measure productivity and increased efficiency in an organization and how this might lead to better service. In an educational setting a Level 4 evaluation may be concerned with the effectiveness and appropriateness of learning and how that affects the ability of the organization to attract high achievers, teachers or learners, grants and sponsorships and academic ranking.

The effective application of Level 4 evaluation can help to ensure a cost justification for the innovation, as well as reinforce the concept of goal achievement and goal clarity. Often the evaluation of the effect of an innovation on an organization is generally cause to assess the mission of that organization.

Conditions necessary for successful evaluation

For a Level 4 evaluation to be successful it must have commitment from staff and senior management.

Level 4 yields qualitative data primarily on behavioural change brought about by an innovation. These changes may have been those intended by the innovation or they may have been incidental. Depending on the questions asked during the evaluation, information may also be obtained on learner reactions to the learning event, on what they felt they learned, and on the results to the organization of these behavioural changes.

Strengths

Level 4 evaluation can be used to assess a variety of learning events, particularly those difficult to measure through objective techniques. It can also be used by itself or in concert with other evaluation approaches and, dependent upon the design of the process and the nature of questions asked in follow up, it can be changed to meet particular information needs and circumstances of an organization. The time required for the evaluation is related to conducting the various interviews and analysing and writing up the results. Basic analytical ability is needed to sort and synthesize the data and draw logical conclusions, but no statistical analysis is required.

Limitations

The application of a Level 4 evaluation can require significant human resources and an additional commitment of effort. However, because people can become naturally protective of various innovations, this may cause a 'fear of cancellation syndrome' that could influence the true response to the evaluation. Also, its high cost may cause the organization to avoid an evaluation of this nature.

A Level 4 evaluation can be costly to put in place.

The time required for interviewing and analysis is often a serious concern. If questionnaires are used, time may limit both the quality and the quantity of response. While a Level 4 evaluation can raise concern for those areas needing improvement, additional data will have to be gathered if discontinuing the innovation is to be considered.

CONTEXT OF THE EVALUATION

The context of the evaluation at Levels 1, 2 and 3 should be seen as one of improvement rather than effectiveness, whereby the information you gather is used to affect ongoing learning events. At Level 4, however, the context should be one of effectiveness based on the impact of the innovation on the organization.

Evaluation questions

The evaluation questions you formulate should be derived from your learning event documentation.

Data collection

Data collection can take place using adapted or already developed information collection instruments. The collection techniques you can use include rating scales, observation, interview and questionnaire.

Data analysis

Your data analysis should seek to make order out of the collection of diverse facts and data gathered. The analysis should accurately communicate the nature of the reaction that needs to be described. It should summarize information, describe how seriously to regard the observations and help determine the amount of relationship among sets of data.

Reporting evaluation information

Finally your evaluation report should detail the instruments you used to gather the data as well as the relevance and quality of your instruments. The rate of progress of that being evaluated should also be described, along with a prediction for its success based on observed progress. The features that appear to promote or hinder progress and your recommendations for improvement will also form an important part of your report.

A Level 4 evaluation is an important process that you need to carry out with a clarity of purpose enough to give those concerned with the innovation an understanding of how it might be improved.

CONCLUSION

An evaluation can be carried out using a number of techniques in a variety of settings. For your evaluation to be successful it is important that you see its context as one of both improvement and effectiveness, depending on the level it is being carried out. It is also important that your evaluation questions are not developed in isolation. Your data collection can take place using standardized collection instruments or you can develop your own. Any subsequent data analysis should accurately describe and summarize all the information you have gathered. Finally, your evaluation report should detail all the features of the learning event that appear to promote or hinder progress.

Chapter 2

Assessing The Learning Event

► SUMMARY ◄

An educational evaluation can be used to assist you, the evaluator, to determine a range of things about the learning event that is taking place or has just been completed. This chapter reviews each of the areas typically assessed during a 'reaction' assessment, namely the quality of the classroom environment, the teacher, the course materials, the use of media, various delivery methodologies, the administrative details and the learner's belief as to the overall effectiveness of the event. The chapter then briefly describes the development and administration of three methods of reaction evaluation.

INTRODUCTION

The various curricula and supporting learning materials that are developed by and for teachers are, for the most part, designed to meet specific learning objectives. In meeting these objectives, it is hoped that there will be an impact on the learner in terms of higher achievement. However, in order to determine if a learning event has had the desired impact, some form of evaluation should be conducted.

Evaluation is the systematic collection of various kinds of information to help you to determine what, if any, modifications have to be made to a learning event. In particular a Level 1 or 'reaction' evaluation, as described in the previous chapter, is designed to help you gain insight to the dynamic flavour of the learning event by having the learner respond to questions regarding the classroom environment, the teacher, the course materials, the use of media, various delivery methodologies, administration and their belief as to the overall effectiveness of the event.

This chapter gives a brief description of a possible ideal of each of the above areas of evaluation. These descriptions, by various writers in the field of education and training, are included to provide some insight into the evaluation questions that you will need to develop.

LEVEL 1 EVALUATION OF A LEARNING EVENT

The classroom environment

> 'The experienced teacher observes classroom patterns with the knowledge that there is no one way of teaching. An overall observational conclusion therefore about the quality of a teacher's relationship to the learners in their classroom should be based on noticed events such as the way the learners change from one activity to another or accept and understand the way the learning event is designed.' *Leonard Marsh on being a teacher* (Marsh, 1973).

From the learners' perspective, no matter their age, it's their level of intensity and ability to articulate the perceived problem that will change the classroom environment. Their concern, consciously or unconsciously, will revolve around the physical size of the room and can or does the learning event take place in the way it appears to have been designed? Is the teacher in control, or are things in chaos? They will consider the seating arrangement and its overall flexibility in terms of can they do all that the learning event demands of them, can they see all they want to see and is the room too hot or too cold?

The evaluative method you use will depend on the age and maturity of the learner.

When you are considering evaluation questions in this area you will need to take into account that older learners are able to express themselves directly to specific questions regarding room size, seating arrangement and the like. Thus, the evaluation could be administered in the form of an questionnaire. For the 'younger' learner, questions will have to be couched in less specific terms and possibly revolve around their need to complete tasks set for them by the teacher. Here you may wish to administer your questionnaire in the form of an interview.

The teacher

> 'The teacher is the ultimate key to change and improvement in the learner. No matter what takes place in the name of educational restructuring and the development of national curricula and the like, all are of little value if the teacher is not taken into account. Teachers don't just deliver the learning materials, they design, develop and interpret it as well. It is what teachers think, believe and ultimately do in the classroom that shapes the kind of learning that people get.' *William Louden* (1991) *on the teacher.*

The evaluation questions that you will need to consider revolve around the teacher's ability to interact with the learner and their ability to deliver the learning materials in a way that is meaningful. Questions should ask the learner whether the teacher was able to explain what was going to happen during the learning event and the role that they and the teacher were expected to play.

Questions should also be developed to focus on how the teacher interpreted and used the learning materials and whether they were presented in a way that was stimulating, interesting and helpful. It is very important that other aspects of what happened during the learning event also be described, such as the ability of the teacher to adjust to differences in learning style and abilities. Consideration should be given to whether or not the teacher encouraged active participation, through the use of examples and illustrations, the explanation of concepts and the enthusiastic answering of questions

The course materials

> 'First and foremost you are an educator, be it kindergarten teacher or university professor, and one of your primary concerns is to produce good instructional materials that would not necessarily win awards for outstanding graphic design, but are effective as learning materials.' *Earl Misanchuk* (1992) *on course materials.*

The questions that need to be considered for this part of the evaluation have to do with how well your learning materials - be they tutorial guides, class handouts, laboratory manuals, individualized instruction packages or textbooks - performed in the eyes of the learner. Considerations include how well the materials matched the real world of the learner, was the content organized into manageable amounts, was the sequence from simple to complex and from concrete to abstract, and were the materials were presented in a way that was both interesting and stimulating.

Your evaluation of these materials should include gathering data regarding the relevance of reading, written assignments, and the 'quality' of any tests or final examination. You should take into consideration directions for the tests and examinations, their length and difficulty.

The use of media

> 'Instructional media can be useful. Their primary purpose is to help the teacher teach more effectively, and the purpose of more effective teaching, we should never forget, is to help learners understand what we are trying to teach them.' *Tanya Slaughter* (1990) *on using media.*

Media in education is used primarily to augment the spoken word. There are a wide variety of media in general use in the classroom, ranging from the overhead projector, through 35 mm slides, to video cassettes. In your evaluation you will need to develop questions that relate in general terms to the media used. For example, a question might ask whether the use of the various media was appropriate for the learning event.

Delivery methodologies

> 'If you talk with teachers and observe what they do in the classroom, you will find that some are very effective in their use of lectures, while others like to use discussions to elicit ideas from the learners. Some teachers are very effective in designing both individual and group practice activities, while others can maintain learners' attention by telling stories about their own experiences. However to be an effective teacher you should not focus on any one method to the exclusion of others.' *Walter Dick and Robert Reiser* (1989) *on delivery methodologies.*

Evaluation questions like those in the previous section can be general in nature. Here, however, you should focus on the organization of the learning event, the amount of material covered and time allocated during various parts of the event. Depending upon the nature of the learning event, questions might need to be raised regarding the mix of theory and practice to determine what, if any, skills were learned.

Administrative details

> 'We know, with some precision, the attitudes, the ways of being, which create a learning climate. We have found that teachers can be helped to develop as facilitators of learning. We have found that these facilitative ways are learned most rapidly during events where the administration maintains a facilitative environment.' *Carl Rogers* (1983) *on administration.*

This part of your evaluation should determine the ease or difficulty with which information about the event was available to the learner and the facility in which the event took place. You should also determine how the information regarding the event was first gained by the learner.

The learners' belief as to the overall effectiveness of the event.

> '... note that if the role of education is to produce changes in learners, then someone must decide what changes are possible and what are desirable. Every teacher-learner interaction is based on some implicit conviction on the part of the teacher and the learner about the possibility and desirability of certain changes.' *Bloom, Madaus and Hastings* (1981) *on evaluating to improve learning.*

Your focus in this final part of the evaluation should be on the relevance of the event to the learner. Did they develop the skills they came to learn? Do they now understand the various concepts and principles of the field? And finally, can they apply these principles to other situations?

DEVELOPING YOUR QUESTIONNAIRE

As well as developing questions in each of the preceding areas, there are three other questions that you should consider for use. These are:

1. What did you like best about this learning event?
2. What did you like least about this learning event?
3. What, if anything, would you like to see changed in this learning event?

Answers to questions like these can provide you with a great deal of insight into various aspects of the learning event. However you should remember that these responses are very difficult to analyse and should only be used as an indicator of where problems might lie. Rather than transcribe all the responses verbatim for your evaluation report you may wish to consider developing a number of categories, under each of the three questions, such as lectures, readings, final assignment, tutorials, opportunity to work at own pace, etc and simply placing the total number of respondents who noted that area on the questionnaire next to the appropriate category.

Each of the questionnaires that you devise in each of the evaluative areas can be administered using one of three methodologies.

1. An oral evaluation administered in a classroom setting.
2. A written evaluation also administered in the classroom.
3. Individual interviews with the learners conducted outside of the classroom.

The evaluation can be carried out either during or at the conclusion of the learning event.

METHOD 1: ORAL REACTION IN A CLASS SETTING

Purpose

The purpose of oral reaction is to provide you with an immediate reading of the perceptions of the learners to a learning event.

Methodology

During this evaluation you will be requesting feedback from learners, using either a structured or fairly unstructured interview process. Your interviews should be carried out in a classroom setting when all learners are present.

Be sure to let your learners know about the evaluation you are going to conduct.

Conditions of use

The learners must be prepared for the evaluation by being provided with guidelines as to what kind of information you will be gathering. Remember that you must receive learner feedback without defensive reaction or explanation.

Measures used

When you use this method no measures as such would be used. You would have a checklist of pre-selected areas that are checked off as various comments are solicited.

Personnel

Only you as the evaluator would be involved in this process.

Administration

The most important administrative factor is that all the learners be provided with the opportunity to contribute but that there is no pressure on any one individual. You can use this method early in a learning event if you have some concerns that you feel need to be identified or isolated, or the evaluation can be used to get a general feeling for the group. Collecting oral reaction data can also be used at the conclusion of a learning event. Whatever method you use, your learners should be provided with a short period of time to consider their comments before being asked to vocalize them.

Implications

You should understand that this method could be intimidating for some learners; it is important therefore that you make them feel as 'safe' as possible. Your behaviour will be a major contributor to the learner's sense of security.

Strengths and limitations

The strengths of conducting an oral interview during the course allow:

- an immediate reaction from the learner

- for the learners to vocalize their concerns and to offer suggestions for improvement
- for you to obtain clarification or further information.

The limitations include:

- learners being threatened by the process
- causing you difficulties when seeking to justify behaviours that have been criticized
- the vocal minority that could 'skew' the review
- the perceptions of the immediate period before the oral evaluation that may colour the learner's overall perceptions of the course
- difficulty in trying to systematically cover all desired areas during the evaluation.

The strengths of an oral interview immediately following the course include:

- the sense of importance passed to the learner
- allowing you to ask questions in depth and to clarify answers given by the learners.

The limitations include:

- the time-consuming nature of the process
- a relatively high impact on an institution due to time demands
- the careful preparation that is needed if this method is to be used.

Tables 2.1 and 2.2 provide examples of questions that can be used during interview evaluation.

Table 2.1 *Example of questions that can be used in interview evaluation (adapted from* Evaluating Training Effectiveness *by P Bramley, 1991, p. 130)*

Questions	Probing
What did you hope to get out of the course before you signed up for it?	To find out if expectations were realistic.
How close was the course to meeting with your expectations?	If it was not close, what were the problems?
What were the most useful things that you learned?	Useful for the job you hope to do? In what way was it useful?
What are you doing differently since you have completed the course?	Ask for specific examples; try to connect to learning.
Is there anything else?	
Specific questions can be asked about particular aspects of the course; ask what students thought were its strengths or weaknesses; ask about aspects which were new or had been tried for the first time.	
Is there anything else that you would like to say about the course?	
Is there anything else that we have not talked about that you think we should have?	

Table 2.2 *Example of questions that can be used in interview evaluation (adapted from* The Art and Craft of Course Design, *by T Earl, 1987)*

Questions	Probing
Was there something you felt you needed in this learning experience that you didn't get?	If there was 'something missing' what was it?
Would you recommend this course to someone else?	To whom? Why? Why not?
What was the sharpest memory of this learning experience?	Is this memory a positive one? If not, why not?
How would you rate your learning experience as a whole?	Ask for specific examples regarding effectiveness, value, enjoyment and efficiency.
Is there anything else that you would like to say about the course?	
Is there anything else that we have not talked about that you think we should have?	

METHOD 2: REACTION USING A WRITTEN INSTRUMENT

When you develop a written instrument try to keep it focused and as short as possible.

Purpose

This method uses a prepared questionnaire to focus feedback on those specific areas desired by the evaluation.

Methodology

Here you will be using a standardized questionnaire.

Conditions of use

Your questionnaire should provide for anonymity of the learners. In some situations you might ask a member of the group to collect the questionnaires, place them in an envelope and then return them to you.

A clear determination of the areas of concern to be covered by the evaluation should be made before you design the questionnaire. Also, it will be necessary to make provision for processing the data.

Measures used

Instruments can vary from short-answer to scalar questionnaires. For your evaluation you may want to provide for both since scalar instruments provide ease of compilation and short-answer questions provide learners with room to elaborate. In general the questionnaire should examine a number of areas. These should include: the quality of instruction, media, administration, facilities, delivery methodologies used during the learning event, the pace of the event, and the materials used.

Personnel

You, as the evaluator, and the learners are generally the only parties involved.

Administration

Written instruments can be used at key points during a longer learning event. This provides you with an opportunity to focus on specific areas. It also allows learners to recall specific aspects of the event with more clarity – recollection might be difficult if the event extends over a number of weeks.

Care must be taken not to cause a negative impact on learners with repeated evaluations.

Strengths and limitations

The strengths of this methodology include:

- learners may share information and reactions
- you are not placed in a position of wanting to react and justify the actions of the learners in view of their comments
- you can focus the questionnaire toward specific areas

The limitations include:

- you are unable to solicit additional information except through the use of follow up interviews
- questionnaires without scalar ratings are very difficult to quantify
- learners' reactions may be influenced by the last part of a course more than the entire session.

METHOD 3: INTERVIEWS CONDUCTED OUTSIDE OF THE CLASSROOM

Purpose

The purpose of the individual interview is to conduct in-depth discussions with learners after they have had the opportunity to consider the impact of the learning event.

Methodology

Your interviews can be either individual or group and are conducted away from the location of the learning event. In most cases they are completed after the event but could take place as the event is happening.

Conditions for use

If you are going to use this method the learner will have to be advised as the interviews might take quite some time.

Measures used

For the most part you should structure the interview. This will ensure that you gather all the data you need. You may want to ask probing questions to get more information; try to determine the direction of probing questions beforehand, otherwise you may collect a large amount of unusable data.

Personnel

You can conduct your interviews using all of the learners or you can pick a sample at random. You can conduct the interviews yourself or a third party evaluator could be used.

Administration

Your interviews could take place during the learning event or at a specific period of time afterward. In some cases you may choose to stagger interviews with a random sample of learners over a period of time in order to discover the effects of time on the event's impact.

Implications

Your interviews should be as non-threatening as possible as learners might not be familiar with this method of evaluation. You should ensure that all learners have been advised of the interview in advance and whether all of them are going to be involved.

Strengths and limitations

Strengths of this type of evaluation include:

- Questionnaires can be well thought out and provide valid and reliable data
- As the evaluator you have the opportunity to question the learners in detail and any number of follow up questions can be asked
- The use of the method may result in a feeling of ownership and responsibility by learners as they are being asked to evaluate in retrospect and carefully.

The limitations include:

- The method is extremely time-consuming and work intensive
- Data from unstructured interviews are difficult to compile and generalize from.

For interviews to be valid

- Training in interview techniques is required
- The interview has to be standardized as much as possible.

CONCLUSION

Evaluation is an important part of the educational process. It needs to be carried out with clarity of purpose so as to give those concerned with the development of the learning event an understanding of how the event meets learners' needs. Many evaluation models are available, but a reaction type evaluation appears to be the most useful.

A reaction type evaluation can be carried out using a number of techniques in a variety of settings. For the evaluation to be successful it is important that the context is seen as course improvement rather than course effectiveness. It is also important that evaluation questions are not developed in isolation. Data collection can take place using standardized or specifically designed collection instruments and the subsequent data analysis should accurately describe and summarize the information gathered. Finally, the evaluation report should detail all those features of a learning event that appear to promote or hinder progress.

Chapter 3

Qualitative Assessment

▶ SUMMARY ◀

Is there a notion in education and training that qualitative assessment is in some way inferior to quantitative assessment? Do you consider qualitative assessment a simile for informal assessment? While the two processes of assessment are different, for both qualitative and quantitative assessment to be meaningful a similar rigour is required. The key when collecting qualitative data is to determine the type of data you are going to gather. In making this decision you will have to determine if the data are valid and how the data can be made valid, systematic and reliable.

WHAT ARE THE QUALITATIVE ISSUES?

When collecting qualitative data for assessment it is necessary to determine the data you require and a reliable means of collecting the data.

Many of the difficulties with qualitative information arise when attempts are made to measure the change in learners and in their attitudes, or developments in their creativity. For example, how do you determine the positive changes in a learner's attitudes when it is much easier to determine that a learner has a poor attitude. Monitoring of attitude is done in numerous workshops and classrooms by monitoring certain indicators. A poor attitude could be indicated by poor attendance, sloppy work, disruptive behaviour or failing to come equipped for the session.

Of course there may be other reasons for this type of behaviour that have little to do with the teaching and learning setting; it may be caused by factors such as home and family matters. The question remains, however, how do you deal with this indication of poor attitude?

It is often assumed that quantitative assessment has to do with collecting statistical data such as scores and percentages about the performance of a learner and qualitative data is collected by other means. But statistical data can be used in qualitative assessment.

This chapter sets out some of the issues involved in qualitative assessment: first the issue of setting standards, then gathering reliable information and some issues of verification and corroboration, and finally creativity and group processes.

STANDARDS

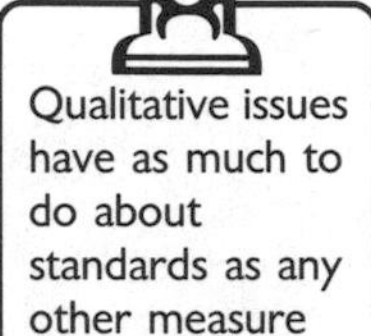

Qualitative issues have as much to do about standards as any other measure of a learner's performance.

When discussing qualitative measures it is appropriate to raise the issue of standards. Unless there are national or agreed standards such as the National Vocational Qualifications in Britain or the common curriculum standards that are emerging through the core curriculum in Australia, then, as in any test leading to assessment, comparisons conducted without standards are questionable.

Standards developed from learning objectives

Do standards developed from statements of learning objectives only give quantifiable indicators? Nothing is further from the truth. A well-structured set of objectives or competency statements will provide information about the indicators that can be used in determining a learner's development as a result of the course. These will include assessment of knowledge gained. But they will also indicate the skills and attitudes to support the knowledge. A close look at curriculum documents may give an indication of standards. In well-constructed objectives there are performance criteria. These set the standard. To reach an assessment of the learner's ability to perform at the set standard you may have to include quantitative as well as qualitative tests to gain the data you require. The same would apply to statements indicating competency.

Meeting standards

In an education and training setting standards are taken to mean performance levels reached and maintained. This will invariably involve a mix of knowledge, attitudes and skills. As the learner progresses the proportional mix may change but the expected outcomes will generally seek higher order levels of performance in subsequent years. In this case higher order skills are equated with age. However, with the move to life-long learners and the need for re-skilling and multi-skilling, an age based chronology may not be appropriate. In some re-skilling, the training involved may require particular learners to upgrade lesser skills before progressing to the new skills training.

There is also the standards related issue that responses by learners to questions and tests are open to interpretation.

- The re-telling of 'facts' may have no relation to the ability of the learner to perform tasks and, therefore, may only be marginally related to the learner meeting the standards required.
- The ability to perform a task is an indicator that the learner knows and can apply that information to an appropriate task. This may fulfil a standard.
- The ability of the learner to perform with attitudes appropriate to the task indicate that the learner has associated with the full range of knowledge, skills and attitudes to comply with standards.

In other words it is what you do and the way that you do it that satisfies the standard. This applies to the academic essay as much as to creative tasks of demonstrating that learning has taken place.

Strategies for applying standards in a qualitative setting

There are several strategies that may be used.

Moderation

There is a strategy of moderation that can reduce the conflict of different standards.

For moderation to work it first requires a group consultation process for teachers. In the area of the arts, for example, teachers come together and discuss their learners' work and compare and contrast it with the work of learners of other teachers in the group. The potential for conflict is great if the process is not handled with tact. Ideally the process is facilitated by people who are known to all the group, while not all the group may know each other initially. The purpose is to examine the learners' work, not the methodology of the teachers. The intention is to take the possible broad spread of ability exhibited in the learners' work and have the teachers agree on the standards they would apply. As a result, a consensus is formed on standards to be applied when similar work is presented by other learners. This focus on the learners' work reflects on the probable wide range of abilities between learners and the consequent variation in their output.

Peer review

Peer review is a process for use by the learners. Two factors are encouraged. The first is fairness, or equity. This happens as each person in the group treats the others as they would expect to be treated themselves. This process can develop the ethics of a professional, rather than professional ethics, within the group. The second factor is increasing the ability of learners to be articulate about their own work and the work of others.

This critical referencing across the group of peers may also lead to the development of the 'critical friend'. As a critical friend, a peer has certain rights, privileges and responsibilities, and must exercise these within a framework established by the person or group seeking critical input. There is the right to express critical opinion; there is a short-lived privilege to stand outside the group to offer that opinion (so long as it falls within the framework established for the session); and there is the most important responsibility of ensuring that the session ends without any unfinished business.

The use of peer review and devices such as a critical friend must not be introduced as a 'good idea'. They must be introduced and discussed within the group and this must be part of the first session. During the first session a plan of forward development, including the number of sessions, is also worked on.

A more traditional form of peer review is the presentation of a tutorial paper by a learner in front of peers. Unfortunately in these days of large numbers and 'pressure cooker' university schedules, the tutorial is often little more than a mini lecture, conducted by the tutor, with the possibility of questions about papers to be presented and marked although these aspects are rarely discussed.

Peer review need not be limited to the upper levels of education. If peer review were introduced into younger levels of schooling, young people might become more articulate about their education and training sooner.

RELIABLE AND VALID INFORMATION

What makes up reliable information? First, let the course documentation be the guide to the information you want. One of the easiest tests of reliable and valid information is to ask colleagues whether, if they were given the information in the course document and the questions you propose to ask, they would consider the learner might be confused. If there is risk of the learner being confused by the questions, this could result in learners providing ambiguous information. This would lead to problems relating to the reliability of information.

Issues of verification and corroboration

Assessing learners is often seen as a 'one task' process. Frequently it is forgotten by both course and materials planners (and teachers for that matter) that as learners progress they will practise the knowledge and skills gained from prior tasks. In reality, as the education and training tasks become more complex, the learners will call on learned skills to complete these more complex tasks. For example, a 'failure' on a new task may indicate the need to 're-learn' some knowledge or skill through remediation. Therefore verification and corroboration are necessary as part of the ongoing education and training process.

A difficult decision you will have to make is whether to make formal or informal records of the information that has been collected. Formal recording of a need for remediation could be seen as a 'demerit' by the learner - whereas, remediation is a way of overcoming an identified lack of knowledge or skills in a specific part of the course.

CREATIVITY AND GROUP PROCESS

Some courses use the development of creativity within group work as part of the education and training process. However, there may be problems when learners prepare and present a group project.

Creativity

When learners prepare and present their creative response in a course that requires this type of response, the learner faces two possible problems. The first is that their creative response does not fit the dominant thinking or idea which should be expressed. The second is that in many areas of creative expression the outcome is produced by a group, even when the idea was conceived by an individual. This produces a blurring of responsibility between the creator and the 'team' that perform the idea, as could happen with a drama or video recording of a student-developed idea.

This opens up the related issue that could confront teachers assessing learners in a group context - the question of how you assess individual members in a group process. Here you will be concerned with assessing learners who have set about a task or a group. You may face the issue of members of the group having worked hard and others who either did not contribute or 'came along for the ride'.

CONCLUSION

There is a mistaken notion that qualitative assessment is in some way inferior to quantitative assessment. While the processes are different, for both qualitative and quantitative assessment to be meaningful a similar rigorous process is required. In both qualitative and quantitative processes the methods must demonstrate validity and reliability. What you have to determine is the type of data you are going to gather, whether the data are valid and how they can be made reliable.

While assessing learners for creativity or their participation in a group process may seem problematic, a considered approach to the process of assessment will result in the collection of reliable, valid and appropriate information on the learner.

There is a belief that every assessment must be supported by evidence. However, it is difficult to quantify the smile on the face of a successful learner. Perhaps you need a camera - after all cameras, like statistics, don't lie, do they?

Chapter 4

Assessment In Each Domain

▶ SUMMARY ◀

Some groups of people involved in education talk about knowledge, skills and attitudes; others use terminology from the taxonomy of the cognitive, affective and the psychomotor domains, while others will use competency statements. But for most learners the question is: Did we pass?, or, What was my mark? For other stakeholders the question is does this person know their work?

INTRODUCTION

What possibilities are there for gathering information to support your evaluation of students' work? In *Planning a Course* the need to plan for assessment of the learners and evaluation of the course was discussed. It was suggested that the tests or tasks you set will give you information, but you still have to perform the assessment. Sometimes the tasks you plan to use become less appropriate as you go through the teaching and learning process and others may strongly influence your judgement of the learner's progress. If you find this happening, note it down; it may be useful anecdotal evidence.

This chapter is in five sections. It first looks at the terminology without getting into a pedantic argument. The next three sections discuss assessment and evaluation in the three domains outlined by Bloom, Madaus and Hastings (1981): cognitive, affective and psychomotor. Finally, the chapter considers reality in the evaluation process.

WHO ASSESSES THE TEACHING AND LEARNING?

It is academic to talk about when we start to learn. By the time the learner reaches school, and through later education, there is a continual process of matching skills with the differing criteria of a variety of people, based on different perceptions of the tasks the learner is performing.

In the education and training setting the criteria used in assessment are often those that are easy to monitor. As a consequence, many tests of a learner's knowledge of a subject fall back on asking the learner to repeat facts, and in a skills-based test the learner is simply required to produce a standard product with minimal defects. And as for attitudes – well they show through in the work, don't they?

It is possible that you thought about the need for assessment when developing the course or materials, but then put off the hard bit ('What am I going to do?') until now? If this is the case read on.

TESTING, ASSESSING AND EVALUATING

Generalizations are often made regarding the use of these terms, and they are often used too loosely. Sometimes they are treated as synonymous when they are not. So how do they differ?

Many teachers use work diaries for administration. Few use them to record learner development.

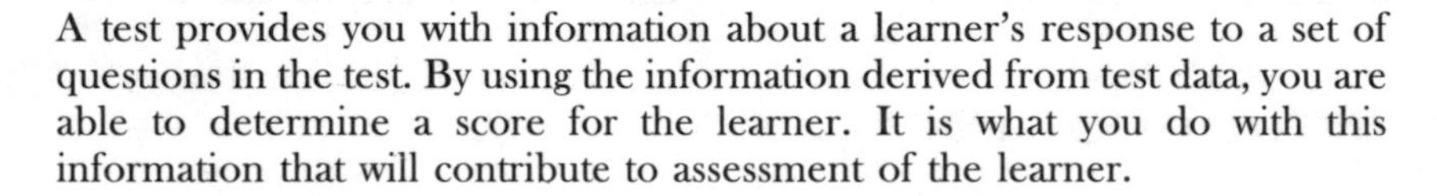

A test provides you with information about a learner's response to a set of questions in the test. By using the information derived from test data, you are able to determine a score for the learner. It is what you do with this information that will contribute to assessment of the learner.

The terms assessment and evaluation are often used interchangeably. However, one of the ways to distinguish them is to understand that typically people are assessed and courses and materials are evaluated. The information provided by a test is assessment information that allows you to determine the standing of the learner.

Because people use these terms in many different ways, when you use them, make sure that the people you are working with understand the context in which they are being used and maintain a consistent use of the terms.

In the next three sections the way people learn is considered in relation to three areas: knowledge, attitudes and skills. Bloom et al. (1981) classified these three areas as cognitive, affective and psychomotor domains. While this work started in 1948, defining and redefining what learners do, how they process information, and the transition from a 'naive' to a sophisticated learner, is still being explored today. It is interesting to consider how far we have moved in the educational debate from developing learning or behavioural objectives to the establishing of key (or core) competencies and the relationship these have with the idea of knowledge as a construct.

THE COGNITIVE DOMAIN

Knowledge

Bloom and his colleagues developed a taxonomy or classification system for educational objectives through which a learner would be required to demonstrate increased sophistication in processing knowledge ie, cognitive skills. The taxonomy was designed to help the field of education deal with curricular and evaluation problems.

As a simple example, Bloom questions what it meant, or signified, when learners recall facts. Does this recall mean they comprehended that information in any other way? For instance, could the learner incorporate that 'new fact' into information to demonstrate that he or she has extended their knowledge?

The purpose of the taxonomy was to make sure that the skills the learner demonstrated in handling knowledge could be tested in a systematic manner. An even more important requirement was that the taxonomy provided test makers with the opportunity of using a hierarchy that would increase the possibility of comparing different tests developed in the same subject but in different schools. A test constructed to determine if facts are learned is different to a test that seeks to test comprehension, or the ability to synthesize or develop a proposal from information already held and newly presented information. A recall test does not demonstrate that higher order skills are involved, or more importantly that the interplay of new information with already held information has caused the learner to synthesize new concepts about their increased knowledge.

How do you develop tests to provide you with information? The answer is to be found in your course documentation. The type of tests you need will be determined by the level or standard of learning the learner must demonstrate and the conditions under which they are expected to perform. If your documentation is complete, these specifications or statements of objectives may well look like competency statements. The reason they will look similar is that objectives and competencies contain the same elements of knowledge, performance criteria and expected outcomes for the learner.

One tendency that you must avoid is testing what is not required to be tested, or testing what has already been demonstrated to be known. In other words, test only what is specified in the objective or competency. You also need to consider the economics of developing, administering and marking a test – the purpose of which is to verify already held knowledge.

THE AFFECTIVE DOMAIN

How do you know when a learner's attitude has changed? Whether it be about the environment, relationships with others, or their responsibilities as employers and employees, the area of the affective domain basically deals with attitudes (Krathwohl *et al*, 1964). At the simplest level it asks that people know the appropriate attitudes; at its most sophisticated it requires a proactive demonstration.

In one sense this places this domain in the area of quality development. If you consider the industrial model of quality, it is a commitment to deliver goods and services to clients that are at, or exceed, the level expected. In an education and training sense this means that teachers and trainers are expected to perform above a predetermined level, as are the learners.

Generally, learners become more skilled at learning as their experience and contact with the learning process develops and expands. But is this parallel with an increasing commitment to quality in their learning?

How does quality fit with developing competencies? How do you develop tests to provide you with the right kind of information? The key yet again is to be found in the objectives or competency statements that form the documentation of the course. Within the affective domain the skills range from the lower order awareness to the high order valuing. However, as stated previously, both qualitative and quantitative improvements in performance would be attributes to be tested. In the previous chapter some of the issues of qualitative assessment were raised.

THE PSYCHOMOTOR DOMAIN

The focus in this domain are the skills associated with dexterity, hand/eye co-ordination, and error reduction in the human use of devices. Of course the proper and safe use of tools requires knowledge of the tools and a responsible attitude towards their use.

In a real sense, judging a learner's ability with psychomotor skills could serve as a summary across the domains. At other times, or with different learners, judging ability could give rise to a need for some detective work if the learner demonstrates less than acceptable skills. You will need to determine whether the low level of skill demonstrated by the learner is due to a lack of knowledge, a poor attitude, or poor skills. How do you go about a remediation process? And how do you develop tests to provide you with information?

The psychomotor skills are about manipulation, but with that manipulation comes selection of resources, stages in the process and safety considerations. And these skills do not always have to be trade related areas. Consider the arrival of word processing with its 'click and drag' attributes that has brought about the need to develop manual skills in areas such as formulating written work or text. These skills change the way materials are written and rewrites are achieved. The skill of being able to produce a typed document is enhanced by the skill of processing those words. These manual skills serve to support the higher order cognitive and affective skills required to develop the writing.

CROSS LINKS AND OBSERVATIONS

When you observe a person carry out a task and are impressed by the outcome, then, generally, you assume you are in the presence of an expert. Someone who has knowledge, skills and the attitude to carry out the task. However, this feeling of the person being an expert also may occur when you see the product of this person's work, without actual observation of the process they go through. For example, you can watch a potter 'throw a pot' and be amazed, or you can see a pot in an art gallery and be equally amazed. In the first instance you would see the skill, concentration and patience required to throw the pot. In the second you see the product and, perhaps even without an understanding of the production process, respond in some way to the object. Indeed, a person who observed the pot being thrown without seeing the pot in the gallery, and another person who only saw the pot in the gallery, could come to similar conclusions about the knowledge, skills and ability of the potter. This, of course, raises the possibility of a potter with bad technique actually being regarded from the pot in the gallery as a producer of good pottery. In reality, the issue is at what point the test is made and who makes the test. If the observer of the potter is another potter, then technique will be important. If the observer in the gallery is a critic, aesthetics will be important.

The task of coming to a decision about the progress of a learner may be difficult and may have many degrees of difficulty. That indicates part of the problem faced by people making judgements about others. Unless these judgements are based on conditions determined in objectives or competency statements, then any assumptions about learners are nonsense - because the parameters and the conditions will vary.

CONCLUSION

People talk about knowledge, skills and attitudes; others use the taxonomy of the cognitive, affective and the psychomotor domains; others use the key competencies. But most learners just ask whether they have passed the course.

Objectives or competency statements will guide you as to the required level of testing, components of the test, expected outcomes and the conditions under which testing should take place. But there is also the less formal information you pick up. Your observations and feedback from learners provide strong influences on your judgement of learners' progress.

Chapter 5

The Iterative Evaluation Cycle

► **SUMMARY** ◄

Each time you offer a course it is the first time for the learners. Two issues arise. The first is about keeping your course up to date. The second has to do with the background of the students that they bring to the course by way of prior learning or experience. However, unless you have means of establishing any prior expertise, then the first time you evaluate students may be at the end of the course. This chapter is about the evaluation or quality control of the course and learning materials

INTRODUCTION

What is meant by the 'iterative cycle'? The four books in this set - planning, developing, delivery and evaluation - are an iterative cycle. This chapter explores the iterative evaluation process. First, it looks at this iterative cycle alongside a model of quality assurance. It then looks at factors that may determine the need for yearly reviews: this includes a short section on 'change for the sake of change'. Finally it will look at the process.

An anecdote

If you are a teacher you have probably heard, seen as a cartoon or read this anecdote before, but it serves an informing purpose. (The original source has been lost in the reality of many staffrooms.)

The scene is a staffroom of a school, college or university. A young teacher enters the staffroom and exclaims:

> '*Teaching is a challenge*!'

A more mature colleague who is leaving the staffroom, turns and makes the parting comment:

> *'Not when you've been teaching for twenty years like I have.'*

The staff room door closes. After a brief pause, another member of staff comments:

> *'Actually, in that person's case, it's been one year's teaching that has been repeated each year for the last twenty.'*

ITERATION AND THE COURSE DEVELOPMENT CYCLE

Figure 5.1 illustrates a version of course development or learning material development and delivery. It is also the model used to develop the four books in this series.

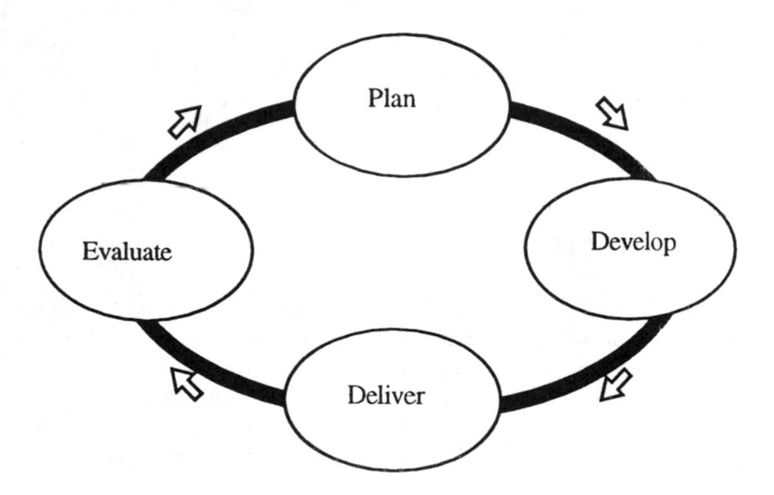

Figure 5.1 *The course development cycle*

The term cycle is misleading because each action taken in the development process might effect, or cause modifications in, the cycle before the cycle is complete. It is probably more realistic to illustrate the process (*not the cycle*) as shown in Figure 5.2.

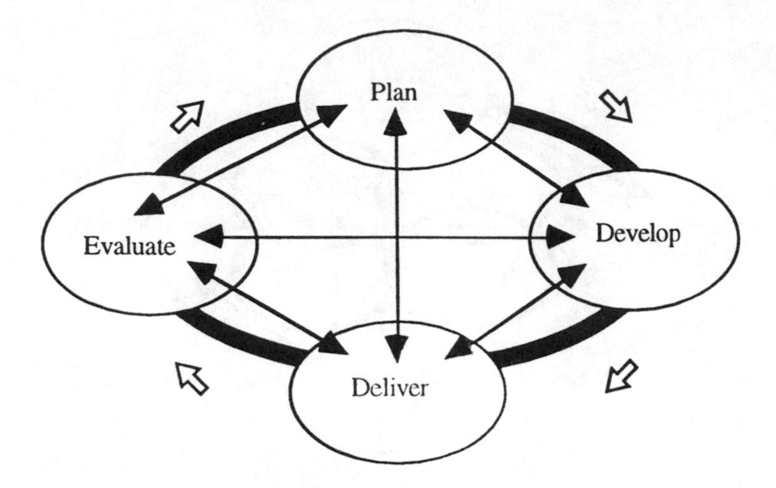

Iteration follows the circle. Reality follows all the arrows.

Figure 5.2 *Iteration in course development*

In theory, iteration follows the circle. In reality, the iterative process is indicated by the arrows. At any time, a development decision may effect not only delivery but also evaluation.

This process also reflects on the Plan, Do, Check and Act (PDCA) cycle for developing quality outcomes in an organization. A point to note is that PDCA is an industrial model, but it can be recognized that the actions that educators and trainers have been taking over the years fit the industrial model which is similar to the iterative process that has been part of curriculum development, evaluation and learning materials improvement.

Accountability is as much about effectiveness and efficiency as it is about learners' progress.

When this process is not fully documented by curriculum developers and teachers, there is often an assumed lack of accountability, but there may be good reasons for this lack of documentation. Teachers often offer time constraints or teaching itself as an excuse for not documenting change - perhaps on the assumption that learners passing the course is the one accountability factor. But lack of documentation may cause problems later if questions are raised about the course or materials.

In the light of the foregoing points it is possible to take the model in Figure 5.2 and align it with the PDCA model of quality assurance.

Figure 5.3 demonstrates the similarities between an educational model of plan, develop, deliver and evaluate (PDDE) and the PDCA industrial model. The processes of PDCA and PDDE are ultimately controlled by humans

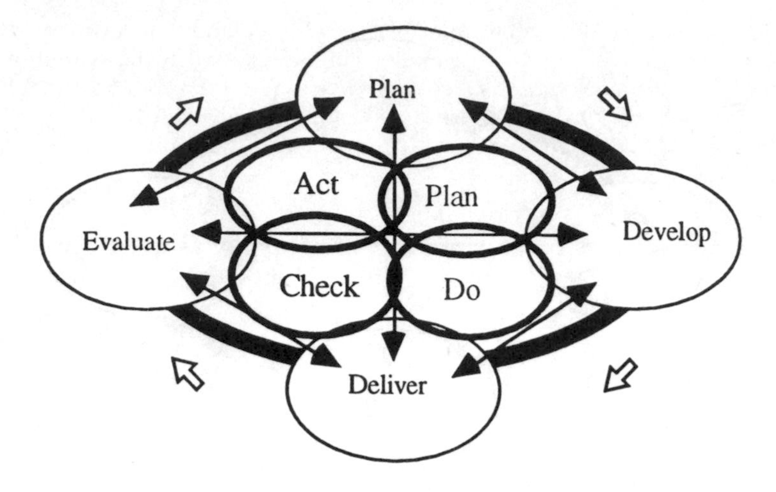

Figure 5.3 *PDCA as part of the iterative process*

and in practical educational and industrial settings some adjustments are possible while the formal process of development and evaluation is taking place. But developers must take account of the 'Hawthorne Effect' - which is caused by interest in the area of development having an effect on people's expectations and outcomes.

Examining or researching in an area is likely to create heightened interest and awareness which could skew the results of the study; this is one aspect of the Hawthorne Effect.

Factors that determine the need for reviews

In the first instance you will need to determine what needs to be considered as part of the review process. In the anecdote at the start of this chapter it was inferred that some teachers taught the same course each year, by inference this assumed that the teacher was:

- ignoring content change
- ignoring the possible use of new technologies to enhance teaching
- not concerned that there may be different capabilities in each year group of learners.

The insensitivity of teachers when comparing learner groups also contains some problematic factors. The first of these is that unless entry level testing is carried out, what comparison is possible on exit level testing? This is, in part, where the industrial model of quality improvement falls down.

In the industrial model each input is tested for suitability to purpose. If a component - for example, a computer chip - is found to be flawed, it is rejected; usually it is found to be cost effective to reject the component rather then complete the product with one which is flawed. But do we consider learners as products? They are not computer chips and we must allow for variations in learners.

The implications of considering the learner as an input component

If you were to consider learners from one level of education (let's say Year 5) under an industrial model, they become the input to Year 6. In an educational model how are learners at the end of year five considered? We make assumptions sometimes to do with future potential, sometimes based on a learner's maturity.

The real questions to ask are: What do I need to evaluate?; What needs to change? Unless these questions are asked you may be faced with change for change sake.

CHANGE FOR THE SAKE OF CHANGE

Maybe it's at the end of the day, sometimes it may be during and at the end of the class, lecture, tutorial or interaction with learners, that teachers appraise the outcome. The review of events is partly to evaluate the outcome as the teacher sees it for the learners; it also serves as a review for the teacher.

For the teacher, there is often the feeling that they will do it differently next time. A real question is: Why do it differently next time? Unless there are issues of content or presentation of content, the learners in the next presentation (which may be next week, next semester, or next year) will be different. If you or the teachers go ahead and make changes on the basis of one presentation, how is it possible to make the comparison between two offerings of the 'same' course? This could lead to complications in the evaluation of the course and learning materials and frustrate the review process.

Planned change

If course designers and developers are realistic, they will have considered the possibility that changes may have to be made at some later date: this may be part of an orderly means of updating the course and materials.

Some aspects of change can be shown against a matrix and strategies and some of the issues that relate to course evaluation and course review.

EVALUATION AS AN ITERATION PROCESS

In the first part of this chapter the notion of an iterative process of evaluation and improvement was discussed. In this part, some of the influences and possible roles or responsibilities of that iterative process are set out in a matrix (Table 5.1).

Table 5.1 *Influences, roles and responsibilities of an iterative process*

Change in content	Plan	Do	Act	Check
Teacher's reaction	This should be identified by subject experts	This has to be a team effort by those responsible for the course	The responsibility of the course team	An up to date course
Student reaction	Students may have an input into identification of subject shortcomings, particularly at postgraduate and industry level courses	Students may have an input to ensure relevance		Satisfied students
Community reaction	In some courses the community may identify needs. Also, there are the inputs and monitoring by professional and trade organizations	There is a need for the community of the learner, and for more mature learners this may include potential employers, to input into course reappraisal	Maybe some responsibility to support the course. This will be the case for courses that directly relate to employment	Greater support from the community – be it parents, caregivers or employers – as they have a stake in the the process

It doesn't matter if you PDCA or PDDE, the main point is to consider the iterative process as part of evaluation.

CONCLUSION

A course familiar to you is new to the students. Keep your course up-to-date. Unless you can establish any prior expertise of the learners, the first time you evaluate may be at the end of the course.

This chapter has been about:

- evaluation or quality control of courses
- exploring the reasons for and means of using an iterative evaluation
- the iterative cycle alongside a model of quality assurance
- factors that determine the need for reviews, including content change
- 'change for the sake of change' and purpose-built change.

Evaluation is an iterative process. The reason for evaluation must be based on documentation and presentation of the course and learning materials, not the whim of a presenter.

Chapter 6

Evaluation For Materials Improvement

SUMMARY

The learners seem to have learned something! What caused the learning to take place? Was it the materials, the delivery strategy or the learning environment that facilitated this process? What things hindered learning? This chapter reviews the various processes for making informed evaluation decisions about the learner regarding behaviour, performance and attitude, with respect to the learning materials you used as part of the learning event.

INTRODUCTION

One of the problems faced by the teacher or trainer is trying to ensure that the learning environment created within the context of the learning materials is the best it can be every time those materials are delivered to the learners. But as all teachers and trainers know, materials which work with one group of learners on one day, might not work with another group the next day. It's only through experience that the teacher is able to 'adjust' the plan to enable better learning to take place.

What makes a learning event a good experience for the learner and the teacher? Is it the environment or just the way it all comes together on that day? What is it that does not work? Is it something in the materials; is it the delivery strategy used by the teacher; or is it just the capriciousness of the learner? To find answers to these perplexing questions it is necessary to evaluate: that is, to make a judgement about the learner, their knowledge, behaviour and performance, and determine what is happening during the learning event when, hopefully, learning is taking place.

This chapter outlines ways to determine whether you are using the right materials, the right delivery strategies, and have created the right learning environment for the learner. It reviews some of the assessment or data gathering methods that can be made before, during and after the learning event, and how you might go about setting up a formal evaluation scheme as part of the learning materials' review process.

REASONS TO ASSESS

Usually you conduct an assessment to help you:

- *plan* what you are going to do as you develop various learning materials, or modify materials after they have been tested with the learner
- *make decisions* about the materials used for learning, the learner using them and the environment in which the learning takes place
- *motivate* the learner to higher achievement when using your learning materials
- *communicate* with the learner and the wider audience.

Evaluation for the purpose of planning

Ask the learners questions about their likes and dislikes in terms of learning materials, what they need to learn, and what they hope to gain from the learning materials.

Evaluation for the purpose of planning or modifying learning materials starts with the collection of data regarding what the learner wants and needs in the learning environment to make it a good or better experience for them. The more you know about the learners, the better will be the learning materials you develop and the learning experience you provide. You might design a short questionnaire to determine the learners' work habits, interests, experiences, learning style and ability to work in a learning environment that is not consistently teacher directed.

Typically when assessing materials for planning or modification purposes you can consider a variety of both formal and informal ways to determine or diagnose the learners' wants and needs. Formal assessment methods can include:

- pre-tests
- entry behaviour tests
- placement tests
- questionnaires.

Informal assessment methods can include:

- observation of learners
- discussions with learners.

Evaluation for the purpose of decision making

When assessing for decision making regarding your learning materials, a number of different formal and informal methods can be considered. The formal methods include:

- checklists
- quizzes
- assignments
- classroom tests

Informal methods include:

- journals
- observation of learners
- comments from and discussions with learners
- assignments.

These methods provide you with data to assist decision making regarding the assignment of learners to special ability groups or remedial classes, or discontinuing a discrete learning event or a complete programme of studies.

Evaluation for the purpose of motivating the learner

Learners respond better when they understand where they are, where they should go next and how they are going to get there.

The typical learner can be provided with three kinds of assessment for the purpose of motivation. The first is the kind of assessment that causes the learner to think more about, or consider more, the materials they are working with. This assessment is often made part of the learning materials in the form of embedded questions to help the learner better determine what they are to focus their attention on as they work through the materials.

The second kind of assessment is in the form of learning objectives that provide the learner with a statement regarding the outcome or result of the learning that is to take place.

Third is the concept of the advanced organizer. The advanced organizer can be designed in such a way as to gain the attention of learners, direct them to the topic, and provide a cognitive structure in which the materials to be learned can be placed. Using this method the information is provided as motivational statements, thereby encouraging the learner to take a positive approach to the acquisition of the required knowledge and encouraging learners to construct logical arguments for or against particular viewpoints.

Motivation can also be in forms less obvious to the learner, in that it is made part of the delivery strategy for a particular learning event. For example, it might include a brainstorming session on a particular topic with the teacher using an opening statement such as: 'For this exercise I want you to think about the ...' Or it might involve a simulation or role play.

Evaluation for the purpose of communicating with the learner

In this area evaluation has to do with the provision of feedback to the learner as they progress through the learning materials. Feedback generally has four different audiences: the learners themselves, their significant others, the institution and the general public.

Learners have a right to know how well they are progressing with the learning materials and in that respect need to receive some form of descriptive information. This description must be positive, informative and written in a way that can be understood by the learner.

People significant to the well-being of the learner such as parents, caregivers and spouses also need feedback and, like that provided to the learner, this feedback should be informative, helpful and specific.

The third body that requires some form of feedback about the learner is the institution. Because this audience often is a peer group there is a tendency for the report to be replete with jargon; however, like the reports to both the learner and others, the emphasis must be on clarity. Unlike the other reports, however, this one could include test scores, observational data and work samples if it is thought necessary.

Finally, reporting to the larger community. It is important that reports help the community better understand the materials the learner is working with in the institution and how that work is appropriate to them and their place in the larger scheme of things.

EVALUATING LEARNING MATERIALS

Planning for evaluation should begin as you start gathering information for the learning materials.

The preceding discussion has concerned itself with the assessment of learning materials during or after the learning event. However, evaluation must also be considered and planned for as part of the procedures in the design and development of learning materials.

Consider a typical project involving the design and development of a series of teacher and learner work books, learner support materials and teaching aids. As part of your initial planning process you will need to consider what evaluation procedures you are going to follow and ask yourself three basic questions regarding the development of evaluation instruments.

- How well did the learning materials contribute to the learners achieving the goals and objectives set out in the materials?

In developing a methodology to answer this question you may have to consider some type of formative or continuous assessment, combined with a summative or final assessment such as a test or examination.

- Are the materials being delivered in an effective and cost effective manner?

To answer this question you will have to consider all the internal and external constraints that impact your materials and make comparisons to other learning materials. This comparison might include: the cost and types of materials, the venue, the time of the day, month or year the materials were delivered, and the type of learner. All of these issues should be examined to ensure that a basis for sound decision making, about the delivery and subsequent retaining of the materials, has been developed.

Are the learners 'happy' with the materials?

This question is not meant to imply that the evaluation should simply ask the learners how they liked the materials. Typically this type of index only measures the 'entertainment' value of a course and the results are sometimes difficult to apply. What needs to be developed to answer this question is a reaction or Level 1 evaluation instrument that asks relevant questions regarding the event itself, facilities, the teacher, media used and materials (see Chapter 2).

EVALUATION DURING A FIELD TRIAL

You should consider conducting a field trial, which is an evaluation procedure in its own right, for any large project, so that your materials can be tried out along with their delivery strategies, particularly if those strategies are in any way different from the norm. A field trial will help determine whether the materials are able to support learning and the learning event itself. As part of the field trial you will need to include the administration of the various assessment tools to gather the relevant data.

Once the trial is completed, the data are analysed – followed by a meeting of interested parties to review the data, determine what, if any, changes are needed, and how and when those changes will be made

ADMINISTRATION OF THE ASSESSMENT TOOLS

Observation during the event

Depending upon the time taken for the learning event, the delivery strategies used and the type of material under scrutiny, you may wish to have an observer in the classroom during the learning event. This person's role would be to report on the various activities taking place; for example, the response of the learner to an activity, the role of the teacher, and how the materials are performing as learning tools.

To help the observer perform this task and to provide continuity to the assessment if there is more than one observer, a questionnaire should be developed. This would provide the observer with a focus for their observation. In the example of what could be a multi-page document shown in Figure 6.1, various questions are made part of an observation tool. The questions asked are subjective in nature and rely on the ability of the observer to focus on the performance of the learner and interpret what is happening. After the observation has been made, the observer is expected to make relevant comments on their observation and the rationale for the score they placed on the scale.

It is important that learners feel at ease during evaluation procedures.

Interview both during and after the event

It is important that as part of the evaluation the learner has the opportunity to express their feelings and opinions about the materials they are using to aid them in learning. The interview should take place in a positive, structured environment where the learner understands the nature of the interview and is able to express their views without penalty.

In order that the interview be properly structured, a series of questions should be developed to focus the learner and to allow other more probing questions to be asked when necessary (see Chapter 2).

Interviews can take place both during the event and/or at its completion. During appropriate breaks as the event is continuing, you may wish to consider posing three simple questions to selected participants (or the whole group if you feel it necessary). These questions are:

1. What have you liked best so far?
2. What have you liked least so far?
3. What things could/should be improved?

These questions can be asked of learners of all ages simply by rephrasing them as necessary. Some learners can be asked to respond orally and others on paper, depending upon their age and the part of the event about which information is being sought.

Learner's demonstrated performance

(a) The things I learned previously fit well into these materials.

Somewhat		In part		Good fit
1	**2**	**3**	**4**	**5**

(b) As a learner I am able to understand the objectives and organization of these materials.

Somewhat		In part		High understanding
1	**2**	**3**	**4**	**5**

(c) The activities suggested in the learning materials helped me to achieve the learning objectives.

Somewhat		In part		High achievement
1	**2**	**3**	**4**	**5**

(d) I found the materials and the suggested learning activities helpful.

Somewhat helpful		Partly helpful		Very helpful
1	**2**	**3**	**4**	**5**

Figure 6.1 *Typical page from an observer questionnaire*

It's important that teachers be part of evaluation procedures – they have feelings too!

If the evaluator is someone other than the teacher, similar questions can be asked of the teacher. Find out what went well from their perspective, and why, and what they might change for the future.

Reaction questionnaires

A reaction questionnaire to a learning event is developed to elicit responses from learners about the quality of the classroom environment, the teacher, the course materials, the use of media, various delivery methodologies, the administrative details and the learners' view of the overall effectiveness of the event (see Chapters 1 and 2). This type of questionnaire can be used both during and after the event and should be asked of both the teacher and the learners.

A teacher reaction questionnaire should seek information in three areas: the content of the learning materials; the methodology or strategy used to deliver the materials; and the facility in which the learning event was held. Opportunity should also be provided to allow the teacher to respond to broad, more general categories, such as suggestions for improvement in the teacher guide(s) and lesson plans, learning materials, media, readings, assignments, exercises and examinations. Figure 6.2 is a typical questionnaire for such purposes.

LEARNING MATERIALS EVALUATION REVIEW

All learning materials are time limited and need to be reviewed and evaluated on a regular basis. It is difficult to say how often this review should happen. Some materials - such as those designed around the topic of trends and developments in computer hardware - are so volatile, it would seem they are obsolete before the learner has the opportunity to interact with them. Other materials are less affected by new developments and can have a shelf life of up to three or even five years. Whatever the shelf life all learning materials should be reviewed at least once every two years in a formal review session. The review should include *all* learning materials. Many institutions will claim to have put in place a review process but this review may cover only the syllabus or the list of topics that the learner has to pass before certification. Learning objectives are sometimes reviewed as part of the process, as are the time allotments for the various topics and, in some cases, the list of subtopics for each major topic.

Time and money are often spent designing and developing learner guides and support materials while materials such as overheads and handouts developed by teachers are largely ignored.

What is not evaluated are materials designed and developed by individual teachers; materials that deliver that topic or sub-topic to the learner. What is being described here is not the delivery strategy as such, or the actual plan the teacher has devised to deliver the material to the learner (although both

General suggestions for materials improvement

Give each of the following an overall rating (eg combined scores for quality, effectiveness, appropriateness) and indicate possible areas where you think improvement might be made.

Teacher guide

Overall Rating (1 = low, 5 = high)

1 2 3 4 5

Note any areas for improvement

Overall Rating (1 = low, 5 = high)

1 2 3 4 5

Note any areas for improvement

Overall Rating (1 = low, 5 = high)

1 2 3 4 5

Note any areas for Improvement

Figure 6.2 *Typical suggestion page of a teacher reaction questionnaire*

of these items should form part of the overall evaluation) but 'other' materials that have been produced, such as:

- readings
- tests and examinations
- work sheets
- tutorial work sheets and associated questions
- procedure sheets.

Usually these items have not been designed and developed as part of the learning materials package by the instructional design team but are left to the individual teacher, subject matter expert or teacher co-ordinator to develop for their classes. Materials should be evaluated on a regular basis to determine their worth. As part of that evaluation a number of fundamental questions have to be posed. These are:

1. Are the materials appropriate for what is being delivered in the classroom?
2. Are the materials appropriate to the needs of the learner, their age, reading level and pre- and co-requisite skills?
3. Do the materials match the goals and objectives set out for the learning event?

Think of a field trial as a dress rehearsal – ironing out kinks so the learning event meets learners' needs.

The first review process could be designed to take place at the end of the field trial portion of the new learning event and thereafter as part of a regular classroom materials review. The various assessment tools should be set up and administered as part of the event at regular intervals during the life cycle of the materials to collect the necessary data. Once data have been analysed a meeting should be convened between the various parties involved with the design, development, and evaluation of the materials. This should include instructional designers, teacher, media specialists and administrators.

At the meeting the participants should follow a set procedure for determining the following:

1. What has taken place with the materials during the learning event?
2. How appropriate were the learning materials?
3. What, in the materials, needs to be changed, modified or replaced?

This procedure might be as follows.

Review the assessment data and identify the problem areas. Based on your data, identifying any so-called problem areas can be relatively simple. What is more difficult, however, is trying to determine the actual cause, and where the problem actually happened. The group will have to agree where the problem is, what it is, and set standards (or use standards already set) for redesigning the problem material. These standards might be based on such items as:

- the layout of the actual learning material on the page
- the format of the materials (Is it standardized across the institution?)
- how the materials are to be physically bound ready for the learner
- how the materials are to be photocopied or printed for the learner
- the kinds and types of test items that should be developed and the test results that are 'desired' by the institution.

Determine tasks to be completed to rectify the problem(s) by determining the problems with the materials. If standards have been correctly set it should be possible to determine what the problem with the material is and how it might be resolved.

If it is determined from the data that learners are having difficulty with completion of a particular set of embedded questions this will need to be investigated. The first and most obvious check would be to review the wording and grammatical structure of the problem questions to make sure that they are clear and unambiguous. This task might be assigned to the original writer of the materials, the instructional designer, or the editor. If all seems well on the grammar side of things, review the objectives for that portion of the material and ensure that the questions are, in fact, related to those objectives and are properly designed to measure that part of the materials. This task should be assigned to the instructional designer. Finally, to try to resolve the problem, review the portion of the material to ensure it is written at a reading level appropriate to the learner. Again, it is the instructional designer who should do this.

Determine the order of tasks to be completed and develop a time frame by preparing a list of each task and a timeline and budget for completion of each task. This final phase of the evaluation process would be carried out by the team leader once the meeting is concluded.

Getting the right person to do the job is essential to the wellbeing of the total review process.

Once the tasks have been listed, they are placed in order. Next, start with the end date and work backwards through each task in turn and determine the time each will require. Once this is complete, a plan for the revision of the materials should be set out in a planning document as shown in Figure 6.3. (See *Planning a Course*, Chapter 3, for a discussion of procedures for planning learning materials.)

The materials design team would also have to determine who will complete each task. It is important that the right person is given the task of revising the learning materials. Giving the materials back to the teacher with few or no guidelines for redesign will very often result in similar 'poor quality' materials being produced.

Type of materials to be revised	Task	Expertise required	Product	When required	Budget
Print-based materials	**Learner workbook** • revise each of the following – summaries – embedded test items – checklists	• Writer • Editor	• Revised learner workbook		

Figure 6.3 *Materials revision planning document*

The kind of expertise needed to revise various types of learning materials is shown in Figure 6.4.

Type of teaching/learning materials to be developed	Expertise required
Print-based materials	• Instructional designer • Subject matter experts • Writer(s) • Editor • Graphic artist • Information entry person • Desktop publisher
Computer-based learning materials	• Instructional designer • Subject matter experts • Writer(s) • Editor • Graphic artist • Computer programmer
Audio visual-based learning materials	• Instructional designer • Subject matter experts • Writer(s) • Script writer • Director • Camera person • Editor

Figure 6.4 *Expertise needed to review and revise learning materials*

Once materials have been revised they should, if there is time to carry this out and money in the budget, be subjected to a second trial to determine whether the revisions had been the right ones. If time or money is not available the materials can be used in the classroom but an observer should be present to determine whether the revised learning materials cause unforeseen changes to the learning environment that are detrimental to the learning process.

WHEN SHOULD THE EVALUATION TAKE PLACE?

The question is often raised regarding the number of times learning materials should be presented to learners before evaluation is carried out, data gathered and, based on those data, changes made to the event, delivery strategies and learning materials.

As noted in the introduction to this chapter, what works with one group of learners on one day might not work with another group the next, so conducting an evaluation and making changes based on one delivery may not be appropriate. But what is appropriate? Are six or ten deliveries necessary to determine what is both right and wrong with the materials or the delivery, or will two be enough? The question is, of course, impossible to answer as factors acting on the teacher and the learners are so many that suggesting a number would not forward the case for evaluation to take place at any level.

The primary consideration is the need for an evaluation to take place during the trial run of a new event or at the first occasion the materials are delivered to the learner, and the necessary changes made after data are collected and analysed. Given the time and budget constraints in modern education, the evaluation might be considered 'superficial' - but it is perhaps the best that teachers and materials designers can hope for. But for all its superficiality the evaluation can, if conducted with care, point to areas of concern and any changes made to enhance the learning environment will benefit the learner.

Some form of evaluation should be considered at least once each year for most learning events but the human resources required to do this might make it an unfeasible undertaking. A more acceptable alternative might be to have *all* learning materials (including teacher notes and handouts) for a particular learning event reviewed *outside* the classroom by subject matter experts, media specialists and instructional designers, and have them compare the materials against the goals and objectives of the materials, the testing and examination criteria, the learners themselves and their needs, institutional standards and norms, and, when necessary, have them revised accordingly.

CONCLUSION

Procedures are required to evaluate learning materials to make them a viable experience for the learner. Evaluation of learning materials should be systematically carried out, using formal and informal assessment tools to ensure that the final result is an appropriate learning experience.

Chapter 7

What Do You Do With The Results?

SUMMARY

This book has focused on formal aspects of evaluation. This chapter discusses aspects associated with following up learners' progress. The process of follow up is concerned with quality issues; and with teachers' interest in the ongoing progress of their learners. However, follow up and checking have another context. Often learners are set projects, homework, assignments or a thesis. How do you give learners independence to complete these tasks, while you monitor the possible outcome in relation to your expectations? How do you balance giving learners independence, with evaluation of how the tasks are progressing?

INTRODUCTION

Although the last chapter in this series of books, this chapter continues to open up issues and suggest strategies to handle those issues associated with gaining optimal feedback on the progress of learners and the viability of a new course and materials. After all, the process of education and training is one of continual improvement.

The main focus of this chapter is on the functions of reporting on learners and the status of this evaluation. The main considerations are as follows:

- What are the learners' expectations? What are the implications of continuous monitoring and checking for the learners?
- What are the implications of learners' ability to access independent

information such as that available through other sources supported by technology and 'out of the control' of teachers, such as the Internet?
- What about the seeming need for many teachers to follow up the progress of their former learners?

This book is about how teachers reach decisions about learners. This chapter is in four sections and deals first with some of the issues; secondly, the records of the learners' work and the audience for that information; thirdly, monitoring; and fourthly, the checking or quality assurance function.

SOME OF THE ISSUES

The ongoing process of gathering information to assist evaluation comes in the form of monitoring or checking learners' progress. This process can be very important for learners; it can also be very frustrating. How do you assist the learner without frustrating him or her? The question is one of accountability.

Then there is the impact of technology on the learning process and the access individual learners have to technology and the way this access may enhance the learners' performance. In the past, technology has been controlled by teachers: but now, some technology is available to learners.

One of the advantages of technology such as mobile phones, modems, facsimile and the Internet it is that one is able to draw upon resources at reasonable cost and within a time frame. This is why the virtual office or Small Office Home Office (SOHO) has developed. Because of the information and work process changes brought about by these technologies, flexible work arrangements have increased – although this has only happened where people and their managers have been able to agree that SOHO is a viable alternative. But how might this technology be applied to education and training?

As technologies are costly and require a support infrastructure, serious questions arise about the availability of equipment on an equitable basis to many of the learners over coming years. This issue is raised here because there are implications in recording and reporting the work that learners do when it is in a 'non-standard' or technology enhanced form. Also, if learners are using technology it may be easier to monitor the work they are doing and the resources they are using.

There are systems in place today that handle many of these issues; there are also systems available that may be the way of the future.

A scenario

Today

In today's class, lecture or tutorial there are learners. Depending on the format of the class and its size, there may have been interaction with some, there may have been conflict with others. When the learners have completed their tests or performed the assessment tasks, you, as teacher, will come to some conclusion about the individuals.

The outcomes of that deliberation could determine the future direction of the learner within the education and training system. While that may sound a bit draconian, in many parts of the world there are other educational options for education and training that do not require traditional forms of education and training. These options exist today in the form of open and flexible learning courses

Tomorrow

Tomorrow is here today. As this book is being written it is possible to say that the options learners had yesterday (read 'Today' above) will be different: also, at the present time, there is much hype about the 'infobahn' of the Internet. It is true that more information is becoming available in the public domain of the Internet.

Three questions or issues need to be considered. The first two are of interest in the overall debate on availability of information. The third is critical in terms of follow-up and checking of learners' work.

1. How long will it be before the Internet is totally privatized? After all, many people in industry or as private users already subscribe to the Internet.
2. How long will it take for a large number of people to realize that the Internet is a good messaging system between groups such as researchers (the original intent) but is being swamped by information that is more economical to distribute to aficionados in print or video form by 'snail' mail (ie the postal system)?
3. When and how will institutions recognize learner-initiated learning via technology such as the Internet? There are examples where teachers and learners are using the Internet as a source of information and incorporating that into a formal learning setting. By extension, the question becomes one of how do teachers and institutions recognize the learning that takes place when a learner, on their own, explores the knowledge on the Internet or through other resources such as libraries and develops their own responses.

(There are many examples of the use of the Internet within certain courses of institutions with open learning/flexible and distance education courses.)

RECORDS OF LEARNERS' WORK

All four books in the series discuss the collection of data from tests, assignments and examinations to provide information from evaluating the performance of learners.

Once you have collected the learners' results what do they mean to you and how do you make them meaningful to others? You have collected this data and come to conclusions - but what do you do with the results? The submission of results for recording is one thing, but there are further considerations. There may be statutory requirements, or other reporting requirements that are the dictates of local 'clients'.

The need to develop means of reporting were mentioned in the first book, *Planning a Course*. It is important that you consider the learners, the community of the learners and the course itself. There are also evaluation issues, when the costs need to be considered and reported. But for the moment the need is reporting to the learner, the community of the learner and to collect information on the course.

Reporting to the learners

In most cases learners want to be told whether they have passed. In some cases, the learner may want to know if their pass was better or worse than a fellow learner. This 'spirit of competition' is fostered by the need to get high marks to enter 'prestige' courses.

Reporting to the community of the learner

As parents or caregivers we often are called upon for advice on how to handle topics set as assignments or homework. Fortunately, as children progress through their education there comes a point where their knowledge of a topic exceeds that of the parent or caregiver and the calls for help gradually fall away. Until that point is reached the process is one of despair and angst until the project or assignment is finally submitted. Parents and caregivers then wait for the mark and when it comes they often wonder how many you earned.

Reporting to teachers

A similar situation exists with teaching. How much help can you give before the work becomes yours and the learner's contribution is reduced to that of your assistant? To avoid this you must be aware of what it is you are doing, the extent to which you have taken over the process, and the degree to which you are denying the learner opportunity to experience the full range of activities set for them.

Of course there is also the learners 'right' to fail. In part this is fraught with difficulties; not least of these is the ego bruising and even cultural stigma that may be associated with failure.

It is very difficult to learn by mistakes in a culture that sees a mistake as a failure in both the learner and the teacher.

If there is to be failure, it should be put into a perspective that enables the learner and the community to see failure for what it is - an inability to reach a set of criteria at this stage or point in time. It should also indicate to the learner the process they must undertake to bring themself to the required standard.

It should be possible to minimize any bad effect of failure by putting it in the correct perspective. Firstly, failure should be seen as a chance to analyse what went wrong and re-do those aspects to reach a more satisfactory outcome. Secondly, failure should be seen by teachers as a chance to review their processes to identify any contributing factors that could be eliminated. These could range from lack of preparation by the learner, including poor background information, to poor task strategies used by the learner. Some of these you may be able to avoid or minimize during the task process if you are monitoring the learner's activity. An evaluation of the teaching processes and strategies involved should show that these did not contribute to the failure of a learner.

Reporting to the community

The results that the community want may be 'Did the learner pass?' However, increasingly the concerns of the community are those of the learner's performance in relation to learners in similar schools, colleges and universities. This is linked to the potential for employment of the learner as an immediate or long-term result of taking part in the course.

Results about the course

You will also need to collect results about the course. These will need to be fed back from the learners, the teachers, and the community. You will need to determine the instruments you will use.

Some options on reporting

Learners want to know how they are progressing. Young learners and more mature learners have a 'feel' about their progress but they need this to be reinforced by feedback from teachers.

At the simplest level feedback could be in the form of a comment. This type of feedback happens all the time in classrooms and tutorials when teachers are able to reinforce comments of learners. Comments such as: 'That's a good point' are indicators to learners of their ability. More importantly, a comment such as: 'You have seen the issue and related it to the topic because you have argued ...' (while convoluted) not only indicates to the learner that you have taken their point and reinforced their learning, but also indicates to other learners who may be thinking similar thoughts that they are on the right track. Such comments may also indicate to learners who are struggling with the problem how they should be working.

At a more complex level the feedback may be in the form of a mark. However, this may create problems when learners have to interpret the mark in relation to their overall progress. For example, a mark of 9 out of 10 looks impressive but the mark takes on a different perspective if the 9/10 is for fifty per cent of the course or for five per cent. Teachers should learn how to describe 'marks' so that all interested parties can quickly and easily determine their relative standing in a group. For example, ranking tenth in a class of 30 is fairly high, but not in a group of ten. To overcome the problem caused by variations in group size, scores can be converted to percentile ranks, which indicate position in a group in terms of the percentage of other students scoring lower. Raw scores are thus put on a scale that has the same meaning with different size groups. For many teachers it is often desirable to only describe a set of scores in brief form. This can be done by computing two measures: the average score, or measure of central tendency, and the spread of the scores, or the measure of variability.

The three common types of measures of central tendency are the median, the mean and the mode. The median, or counting average, is determined by arranging the scores in order of size and counting up to the mid-point. If there is an even number of values the median is the average of the two central values. The mean or arithmetic average is determined by adding all the scores in a set and dividing by the total number of scores. The mode is the most frequently occurring score and is determined by inspecting the frequency for each score.

The spread or variability of a set of scores can be described by using the range and the standard deviation. The range is the interval between the highest and the lowest score. The standard deviation is an average of the degree to which the scores in a set deviate from the mean.

Sending results

The report card and posting of results are traditional means of reporting the progress of learners to the wider community. At the school level this is supplemented with parent-teacher afternoons or evenings and sometimes by more qualitative reporting.

Qualitative reporting generally takes the form of a short narrative on the progress of the learner. Often it contains a statement about an aspect of the learner's work which the learner should try and improve. While these statements may be informative it should be recognized that in many communities the type of support that would allow a learner to overcome these difficulties may not be available.

Teachers and course developers have to remember that in the community of the learner many members will be long out of school and that the form of schooling has changed. For those community members who have had further education and training, the majority of experiences will be job related. Teachers have to carry in the back of their minds that many in the community still see education as a means to a job.

While many in the community have coped with job changes, they seem unable to acknowledge that education and training, and retraining, are a life-long process. Therefore, teachers and trainers need to be clear about the reporting process they are undertaking. Unless there is a very clear relationship between the course of study and employment it is very difficult to correlate success in a course and employment.

You will need to consider the possible outcomes and any possible misinterpretations of reporting to the community of the learner.

MONITORING

Whether in the laboratory, the library, the classroom, or on a field trip, part of the teaching function is to monitor the progress of learners. This is to make sure that the learners are on the right track. During this monitoring you will be able to determine whether the learners have followed or are following instructions and whether the likely outcome will be achieved. This is an indicator of the learner achieving success, although there may be degrees of success between learners. So monitoring for success in task completion is sound practice. However, there may come a point where this monitoring intrudes on the work of the student and this can cause problems with the information you are gathering for evaluation.

If follow up is a process that allows you to check on the progress of the learner then how does it differ from monitoring? Monitoring is a process that alerts you to problems and allows you to intervene to avert a problem that would otherwise only be found at follow up. This intervention can happen at several levels.

At the first level there is the monitoring of the 'factual material' and do the learners know it and, more importantly, are they consistent in using it? At this level it is easy to test for knowledge, but that is an indicator of knowledge only at the time of the test. The process of monitoring provides points of reference to the ongoing use of the knowledge.

Then there is the monitoring for correct practice. Without the need for constant surveillance, monitoring will provide information on the learner's continual correct performance of tasks.

Thirdly there is the concept of fading. Fading is a process where the subject expert (teacher) allows the learner to gradually assume the responsibilities of the expert. Undertaken over a period of time, it is the process that sees the subject expert reduce their role in teaching the learner while supervising the learner as the learner becomes a subject expert. This takes time. A central point of this process is that the teacher may maintain contact with the learner for a period beyond that of the formal course.

QUALITY

Elsewhere the issues of iterative evaluation and quality have been discussed. Three considerations remain.

Just checking

Once a learner has passed part or all of the new course and the associated materials, is there a need for you to check or are you insulting the learner and perhaps showing lack of security in your ability to educate or train?

Follow up as after sales service

Is after sales service a consideration in education? If it is, how have you planned for it in your course and materials?

Reporting on budget matters

It may not be an educational issue but the costs of planning, developing, delivery and evaluation of a new course and materials are important. Budget estimates at the start of a project that are approved should become real working parameters. In most economies the ability to accommodate a change in budget involves considerable effort and stress.

Under budget. There are settings where new courses and materials come in under budget. In some educational and training settings in the past, this was seen as a bad situation.

Over budget. In many past settings it was expected that most new programmes and materials would come in over budget. The reasons for this would be many and varied.

It's clearly advisable in today's education and training climate to come in *on* budget. To do this you will need to constantly monitor expenditure. Focus on the 'must have' items in the budget, rather than the 'nice to have' items that turn up.

CONCLUSION

When reporting on new programmes and materials in education and training, the stakeholders are the learners, their community and the educational and training community. You will need to devise a reporting strategy for this diverse group and it is important that you determine the type of information required. Learners want to know? Parents and caregivers want to know? And the wider community?

Chapter 8

Evaluation: Finishing or Starting Point?

► **SUMMARY** 

This final chapter reinforces several aspects of the evaluation of course and material development. Discussions in this book and the others in this series touched on these issues. Here we point out some of the specific actions you could consider at the evaluation stage. The purpose of these actions is to improve the product you have worked so hard to develop. Of course, effective evaluation can only be based on good documentation.

INTRODUCTION

This chapter first uses the iterative cycle of quality assurance outlined in Chapter 5 to suggest some possible quality control mechanisms. Secondly, it discusses the need for staff development that may arise from the evaluation. Finally, it reviews the need for initiatives in course development to align with emerging national standards for curriculum in both education and training.

QUALITY ASSURANCE AND QUALITY CONTROL

In Chapter 5 the iterative cycle of course or materials improvement was presented, and Figure 5.1 on page 48 showed the complex interaction between the development, design and delivery of courses, the provision of appropriate and effective courses and course materials, and the means of evaluating the outcomes. There is an underlying expectation that the actions carried out in the materials development cycle contribute to the purpose and activities of quality assurance and the quality control tools that are used to provide data for quality assurance.

However, there is a need to be clear about quality assurance and quality control as used in the evaluation process. The two terms are often seen as synonymous, but this is far from being the case. At the simplest level quality assurance suggests that the activity has a quality focus. This is a valid focus. However, this should not be confused with quality control, which entails the use of particular tools designed to collect information. It is through responses given, and their analysis, that it becomes possible to demonstrate that a quality product was the outcome. For example, in an industrial setting it is relatively easy to determine that the outcome of certain actions on raw materials resulted in a quality product. Is the computer chip in the correct place on the board? Is the thickness of the steel slab within tolerance limits after rolling? In each example there are tests that can be done and checklists or tick sheets developed to collect this information. Of course, there may be other aspects of the job that need to be tested to make sure the product is fit for purpose. Does the chip work after it is installed in the correct position? Is the steel slab the correct width within tolerances while meeting the thickness requirements? This might be handled by other checklists. Whatever the form of the checklist these are based on providing information to help document a quality process.

When you need to determine what the quality focus is at the evaluation stage of your learning materials you will have to answer the questions below. Remember that quality is a client-oriented focus, determined by what the client wants or needs. At the evaluation stage, the main question to be addressed relates to client expectation and need, where the client may be a learner, a teacher, the institution or the community. You should have thought about the wants and needs of evaluation at the planning stage and during the development process. Now it is timely to re-examine the original documentation to make sure that the client needs are addressed in the evaluation.

What did the client express as a want or a need from the evaluation?

By now you will be aware that sometimes what a client *wants* is not what they *need*. The client may have an idea about the process of evaluating the course and materials and the expected outcomes, but this will be based on their prior experience.

If you attempt an innovative evaluation process, there will be one of three reactions. The first is to reject your proposal for evaluation, because your suggestion does not meet with their view of the process. The second reaction is enthusiasm for the evaluation process, but there is potential for enthusiasm to override the needs of course and materials evaluation that would be fit for purpose with a course and materials evaluation that is excessive for the purpose. It is not difficult to see why the two opposite reactions occur. In the first case entrenched ideas rule. In the second, enthusiasm overrules an appropriate response for a course or materials evaluation. The third reaction is that your proposal for evaluation is accepted as is. In each case you should be able to refer back to the initial documentation to support your suggested evaluation strategy.

There are also the working aspects of the evaluation.

Project specification

The curriculum documents developed to support the course and materials must be sanctioned and available to verify the evaluation strategy (see *Planning a Course*). Within that documentation should be the evaluation and reporting indicators to show that the learning objectives have been achieved, exceeded or not met. The task of evaluation and the subsequent report preparation will be based on these indicators, which might include comparison of learner outcomes, time and cost factors and teacher satisfaction with any previous courses and the new course or materials.

Monitoring the process (job aids created)

A further source of information on the effectiveness of new course or course materials can be found in the way teachers work with the course/materials. Most effective teachers are also record keepers and facilitators. The need for them to record events extends beyond keeping attendance sheets (depending on subject content) to skill audits of learners in practical subjects to mentoring in other subject areas. Alongside the job aids developed for the course and materials, many teachers develop their own job aids to assist them in recording student progress and their own progress in presenting the content.

Compare a job aid for quality assurance and one for quality control. A job aid as a quality document dealing with one lesson in a course might look something like Figure 8.1. This table assumes that you have considered the tools to collect the information. As outlined in this series of books the need to collect this type of information has been promoted.

Now look at the quality control sheet in Figure 8.2. A different set of questions are generated if you are ensuring quality control, and could take the form of a checklist. For instance, a teacher might develop a checklist to ensure they have the materials they need as they walk into the classroom. A quality control sheet such as Figure 8.2 will help the teacher to be in control of the classroom situation.

Quality issues	Quality measures
What knowledge, skills and attitudes are expected of the learner when they enter the course or start using the materials?	How is the teacher expected to determine this?
What are the strategies to be used in this lesson from the course documentation?	How is the outcome for the learners of the use of these strategies to be determined?
Are other strategies applicable?	How is the use of these strategies to be documented?
One lesson generally is only a part of a course: how is continuity from this lesson to the next to be carried out?	What issues in this lesson need to be reinforced from previous lessons?
A lesson may not require a formal testing process.	If this lesson does not contain a formal evaluation task, what are the indicators that you will be looking for, to determine that the learners are learning?
After the lesson or use of these materials you are evaluating, what are the outcomes for the learners?	What information needs to be collected to show that the learners achieved the outcome?

Figure 8.1 *Quality job aid*

Lesson checklist

Lesson ______________________________

What do I need for this
lesson/class/tutorial/demonstration

☐ Text books. Which ones? ____________________

☐ Handouts to learners
prepared
need to be prepared

☐ Overhead transparencies/videos

☐ Demonstration material or other teaching aids

☐ Experiment material for learners to use

Other resources required

____

____

Figure 8.2 *Quality control sheet*

A different version of the checklist might have information about the topic of the lesson, or the questions may just need the headings such as:

Needed	Have	Not needed

It maybe that these tools are developed by the individual teacher and meet only that teacher's needs. However, you should be looking at the job aid to determine whether it can serve the purpose of collecting information on aspects of the course or materials that are currently being reported. In other words, these 'informal' tools may serve as a source of information for your evaluation. But teacher tools need to be handled with care: they are working records that the teacher may have developed for use in preparing a report for and about each learner. Your interest is in the evaluation of the course and the learning materials and with the *outcomes* for the learners. You will have to determine how you use specific information towards the goal of reporting on the effectiveness of the course and materials and the outcomes for learners and teachers.

Outcome – fit for purpose

If the course specification, development and materials development have been put through the rigorous consultation, documentation and development process outlined in this series of books, you will have enough information to assert that the course and materials are fit for purpose. The evaluation purpose should be designed to provide information from which you and the stakeholders can arrive at decisions about the quality of the course and the materials.

However, during the evaluation and report preparation activities, you should recognize that, no matter how close the working relationship of the team might be, it is possible that someone in the team (one of the clients, or other participants) may have gathered information on the course or materials that is beyond the evaluation that was planned. For example, a teacher may have collected information on learners about their enjoyment of using the materials. This information may not have been considered in the original evaluation plan for the course and materials development. If this information is available to you and the team, you will have to determine how it will be incorporated into the final evaluation report. This section is to remind you that you need to keep the original intent in focus. You must constantly 'revisit' your original documentation. After all, it may be some time since it was drafted and you have since been occupied with development tasks and delivery issues. Now at evaluation you should be very sure what it was that you wanted to evaluate.

STAFF DEVELOPMENT

The evaluation stage is a good time to reflect on staff development matters. In the enthusiasm for a new initiative in education and training, it is possible that staff overestimate their ability to contribute to the process. As you are evaluating the feedback on the course and materials, consider the ability of staff to deliver the learning materials. Some of the areas you may need to examine are:

- consultation process
- induction
- training

- outsourcing of training or that part of the job that lacks expertise in your team.

How was the consultation process handled?

Some of the feedback that you might want to collect will include information on:

- *The original need must be verified.* One of the main concerns is to reinforce that the perceived need for the course and materials was accurately identified.
- *The key players/stakeholders.* There is a need to make sure that these people see the course and materials as serving their purpose and to gain their support for continuing. You may need to check that all the appropriate people were consulted.
- *The learner's perception of the suitability of the course or materials.* There is a problem of being able to track learners over time and particularly learners' reactions to the course this year and to the course as offered (eg, modified because of technology). If it is possible to track learners, they will be a valuable source of information when course or material revision is needed at a later date. There is also the probability that even over a short period of time technology will change and this can create problems when trying to maintain course relevance.

How was the induction process handled?

When new courses and materials are developed it is possible that the development team are inducted into the development process, but then the delivery personnel only receive training on the materials. When this happens the delivery personnel may miss out on the grounding information that forms the basis of the course and materials. The difference between induction and training and the development and delivery of courses and materials is important. The distinction between induction and training has to do with the level of commitment.

- **Induction**
  The induction process involves an indepth grounding in both content and process. It is based on the background information gathered for the course, the reason for using selected teaching and learning strategies, with the eventual commitment by the teacher to an agreed set of events when using the course and materials.
- **Training**
  Training is a process undertaken by teachers to enable them to present a course or materials. In many cases assumptions are made about the level of expertise of the teacher as a 'trainee'. It may be assumed that there is commitment to use the course and materials, but the training could be

wasted if there is little commitment to using the material by the trainee. You might need to examine the causes of limited commitment. Possibly the trainee is not convinced of the value of the training to them. At the same time, many 'professionals' only need training; they are practitioners and therefore do not need induction (see Chapter 3 of *Preparing a Course*).

At the evaluation level it is important to gain information on the induction/training process to provide information on how teachers are using the materials. The evaluation information you collect could indicate to you differing needs for induction and training among the people who use the course and materials.

How was the training process handled?

Given your involvement in the development of the learning materials and documentation, and the consultation, it is likely that you (and any support) can develop an induction and training process. You and the material development team have a strong commitment to the course and materials and should be capable of seeing the needs of those who are going to implement the project.

Outside expertise

In some areas of development of the expertise of the delivery personnel it may be possible to identify areas of expertise that are lacking, which could be overcome by using external sources. For instance, this could arise in counselling of learners or consultation with parents and community.

In terms of staff development, one of the key areas of staff training is the integration of the 'national' standards, 'key' competencies and 'quality frameworks' that many educational and training organizations are putting in place as a consequence of political and economic requirements.

COMPLIANCE WITH NATIONAL STANDARDS

In many countries around the world, government-sponsored bodies involving employer organizations, unions and the education and training organizations are developing standards. These standards apply to educational subjects, such as maths or English, as well as vocational training. Indeed, the very development of these standards, particularly at the later years of a student's education, is blurring the traditional boundaries between education and training. One reason for this is that now there are accepted standards in both education and training for identification of the competencies a student needs to satisfy and to pass academic/educational courses and a set of standards a person needs to be eligible for a job. As an example, it is now recognized that an ability to communicate is part of education and training and that there are various levels of communication skills. During both education and training these skills need to be developed and tested.

The second reason is the shift from training for a job to 'lifelong learning', which is caused by the changes in jobs through technological advance in the workplace and the resulting need to upgrade skills to remain employable in the 'new' work setting. Taking each in turn, there are implications for evaluation.

- *Identification of the competencies a person needs in education and for a job*
  In both the educational and vocational training settings the move is away from specialization in education and in specific job training. In job training the demarcation between jobs skills is often seen as unproductive. This has led to demands for multi-skilled and adaptable employees able to respond to need. In the typical work setting the progressive accumulation of skills is at odds with the individual employee's ability to respond to a need for their particular aptitudes and expertise.

- *The shift from training for a job to lifelong learning*
  If the future of work and, by default, education and training is to be one of constant change, and this change is against a set of skills and requirements or competencies that may change in part or in total, then the ramifications for any evaluation process are important. An evaluation by its very nature is a looking-back process, what happened and what were the successes and failures? There is an expectation that you will be able to put the information from the evaluation into practice the next time the course is offered. While that may be the case, you should also note that in some areas of education and training although change will be gradual, there will be change. In other areas, change will be more rapid and perhaps erratic. Technology in the form of computers, new materials for industrial fabrication or revised methods of working in education will cause problems for the view you take on the course and materials and the recommendations that result from the evaluation.

THE PROCESS 'AFTER' EVALUATION

Course planning and course material design, development and delivery take place within a given context of education and training. Increasingly, there is the wider context of standards established by national educational and training organizations and organizations involved in quality assurance. As a result there is a need to use

- effective quality assurance processes
- appropriate staff development
- course development that complies with existing and emerging national standards.

The point about existing and emerging standards is of particular importance. During the time-consuming process of planning and developing and delivery of a course and materials, the very ground (on which the course and materials are based) is changing because of factors such as: changes in technology; and new initiatives announced by governments and government agencies.

As a person or group involved in evaluation, it is important to refer back to the original evaluation plan developed at the planning stage. This will allow you to account for, or discount, factors such as evaluation in technology and the possible content change in the course or methodological changes as a result of evolutions in technology, and include these factors in the evaluation reports. But having done all that, there may still need to be a debriefing process. This may be a process beyond your evaluation strategy.

A debriefing reaffirms the objectives, assesses the extent to which they were achieved, assesses the outcomes and suggests any further action.

Many of the actions taken so far in the planning, development, delivery and evaluation would be part of a debrief. However, you will need to consider if there is to be a debrief and whether it is to be informal or formal in nature. Some of these considerations would be:

- *The course development and resulting material*
  Course and material development on a local scale would be handled differently to regional or national course and material development. You will have to be the judge.
- *The contributors to the process of planning, development, delivery and evaluation*
  Again, there are considerations of size of course and numbers of people involved. If only a small group was involved then much of the debriefing will possibly happen on a personal level. However, if other authorities are involved, such as government agencies, there will probably need to be a more formal debrief. On large-scale planning, development, delivery and evaluation there will almost definitely need to be a formal and probably comprehensive debrief.
- *The audience that has an interest in the outcome*
  This audience will consist of the key planners and stakeholders and the scope of the project will determine those that need to be involved.

There is also the form of debriefing that results in a party. And that is meant seriously. Having spent all the time and effort on planning, development, delivery and evaluation, and with a successful outcome, there is indeed time to celebrate. It may be difficult if the team is large or where distance is a factor, but if the team was small or local, then think about a social debrief. Remember you and others have given your time and energy. Now your course and material are out there. There is a cause to celebrate, there is also the relief that 'it's all happened' and there could well be a feeling of vacuum ... all that work is now over. But then, there is always the next challenge.

Further Reading

Bloom, B S, Madaus, G F and Hastings, J T (1981) *Evaluation to Improve Learning*, New York: McGraw-Hill.

Bramley, P (1991) *Evaluation Training Effectiveness*, London: McGraw-Hill.

Cartwright, C A and Cartwright, G P (1984) *Developing Observational Skills*, London: McGraw-Hill.

Dick, W and Reiser, R A (1989) *Planning Effective Instruction*, London: Allyn & Bacon.

Earl, T (1987) *The Art and Craft of Course Design*, London: Kogan Page.

Gagné, R M (1977) *Conditions of Learning*, 3rd edn, New York: Holt, Rinehart and Winston.

Goad, T W (1982) *Delivering Effective Training*, San Diego, California: University Associates.

Harlen, W (ed.) (1994) *Enhancing Quality in Assessment*, London: Paul Chapman Publishing Ltd.

Harris, D and Bell, C (1986) *Evaluating and Assessing for Learning*, London: Kogan Page.

Kirkpatrick, D L (1977) 'Evaluating Training Programmes: Evidence vs Proof', *Training and Development Journal*, November, pp.9–12.

Kirkpatrick, D L (1989) 'Evaluation' in *ASTD Handbook of Instructional Technology*, New York: McGraw-Hill.

Krathwohl, D R, Bloom, B S and Masia, B B (1964) *Taxonomy of Educational Objectives. Handbook 2: Affective Domain*, London: David McKay Company.

Long, D G (1990) *Learner Managed Learning*, London: Kogan Page.

Louden, W (1991) *Understanding Teaching*, New York: Teachers College Press.

Mager, R and Pipe, P (1981) *Analyzing Performance Problems*, Belmont, California: Pitman Learning Inc.

Marsh, L (1973) *Being a teacher*, London: A & C Black Ltd.

Misanchuk, E R (1992) *Preparing Instructional Text*, Englewood Cliffs, New Jersey: Educational Technology Publications.

Rogers, C (1983) *Freedom to Learn for the '80s*. London: Charles E. Merrill Publishing Company.

Sax, G (1980) *Principles of Educational and Psychological Measurement and Evaluation*. Belmont, California: Wadsworth Publishing Company.

Slaughter, T M (1990) *Teaching with Media: A guide to selection and use*, University of Melbourne, Victoria: The Centre for the Study of Higher Education.

Ward, C (1980) *Designing a Scheme of Assessment*, London: Stanley Thornes (Publishers) Ltd.

Index